About the Author

Penelope Quest is a graduate of Psychology, Management and
Education with 15 years' experience as a college lecturer. She
began her own journey of personal and spiritual discovery in
the 1970s, eventually developing skills as a clairvoyant and
channel. Starting as a Reiki practitioner in 1991, she became a
Usui Reiki Master in 1994 and a Karuna Reiki™ Master in
1996. A former member of the Reiki Association's Executive
Council in the UK, she has lectured regularly on the complementary therapies' options on nursing degrees and diplomas
in hospitals. Having also studied many other subjects which
promote understanding, personal growth and a holistic view
of the person, she now teaches Reiki and runs workshops and
retreats on other mind-body healing techniques.

Reiki

Piatkus Guides

A PIATKUS GUIDE

Reiki

Penelope Quest

PIATKUS

This book is dedicated to Usui, Hayashi and Takata

This book gives non-specific, general advice and should not
be relied on as a substitute for proper medical consultation.
While all treatments are offered in good faith, the author
and publisher cannot accept responsibility for illness arising
out of the failure to seek medical advice from a doctor.

© 1999 Penelope Quest

First published in 1999 by
Judy Piatkus (Publishers) Ltd
5 Windmill Street, London W1P 1HF

The moral rights of the author have been asserted

A catalogue record for this book is available from the British Library

ISBN 0-7499-1935-3

Designed by Sue Ryall
Illustrations by Zena Flax

Set in 12.5/14 pt Perpetua
Typeset by Action Publishing Technology Limited, Gloucester
Printed & bound in Great Britain by
Mackays of Chatham PLC

Contents

Acknowledgements

My heartfelt thanks and gratitude:

To my Reiki Masters, Kristin Bonney and William Rand, who inspired me and taught me so much.

To the other Reiki Masters who shared their experiences with me, particularly Sean Milligan, Sadie Whelan, Eileen Reilly, Sue McCarter, Carrel Ann Farmer, Phyllis Lei Furumoto and Paul Mitchell.

To all my students and clients, from whom I have learned so much and who have helped to make that learning such fun, notably Marilyn Bryan, Paula Strong, Julie Pearce, Linda Ellison, Susan Dimaline, Christine Ridley, Chris Houghton and Cath Baxter.

To my friends for their ideas, inspiration and belief in me, especially Simon Barlow, Jackie Gleeson, Pam Day and Wendy Monks.

To my mother Irene Harris, my daughter Kathy Roberts and my son Chris Roberts, for all their love, support and encouragement.

Introduction

More and more people are intrigued by and attracted to the idea of hands-on healing. I have always been interested in esoteric and alternative subjects, and began my search for personal and spiritual development in the mid-1970s, studying anything and everything from astrology, cartomancy and graphology to social psychology. One evening in 1990 I attended a lecture on personal growth techniques. The speaker, Kristin Bonney, impressed me. She seemed at ease with herself, so calm and tranquil – and tranquillity was such a rare quality, and so absent from my own life at the time, that I wanted to find out how she achieved it. In conversation afterwards she told me a little bit about Reiki, which she described as a hands-on healing technique which encouraged a sense of relaxation. At the time I was living a frenetic lifestyle as a single parent, college lecturer and Open University student, so it sounded like something to investigate.

I went along to one of Kristin's introductory talks on Reiki, and I found the evening fascinating, not just because I heard more about it, but because I had my first chance to experience it flowing through me. It was amazing. I sat on the floor in front of a Reiki practitioner and while Kristin talked he simply placed his hands on my shoulders. Very quickly I could feel this wonderful flowing softness, gentleness, warmth and tingling flooding my body. I could feel emotions welling up inside even though I felt quite relaxed and peaceful. I could sense its soothing progress down my body, into my legs, and right into my feet and toes. It was the most astonishing sensation, and after only 15 – 20 minutes I felt fantastic. I decided right there and then that Reiki was something I really wanted in my life.

Some months later I attended a weekend Reiki First Degree course. I went along in some trepidation, not sure what to expect. I had always assumed that healers were very special people, born with particular gifts, so surely an ordinary person like myself couldn't become a healer, and certainly not in just a couple of days?

Of course I was proved wrong. I came to realise that we *all* have the potential to be healers. Even by the end of the first day I could feel a lovely warm energy flowing from my hands when I tried to use the Reiki on myself. By the end of the second day I had successfully carried out my first Reiki treatment on one of the other students. It felt wonderful, and I couldn't wait to try it out on my family and friends. Soon I was treating people on a regular basis, fitting appointments into my busy life with surprising ease.

I found I was benefiting enormously from using Reiki on myself, too, and after a year I felt it was time for me to take the Reiki Second Degree. Nothing I could have anticipated would have prepared me for the stunning effects of that course. It was as though the whole world around me had changed – colours were brighter, sounds were sharper, smells and tastes were more intense – as if a veil had been removed and I was seeing the world for the first time. My awareness seemed to be incredibly enhanced, and I felt a tremendous sense of connection to everything around me, from rocks and water, to plants and people.

It felt truly magical. I had taken an enormous leap forward spiritually, and over the weeks and months which followed, as I practised the new skills I had been taught, I discovered that my intuition and psychic abilities were growing rapidly. Over the next few years I became clair-voyant, often 'seeing' inside a client's body so that I could tell what was wrong with them. The first few times were something of a shock – I thought X-ray vision was limited to science fiction stories!

I continued to give Reiki treatments at home, and began to give talks about healing to interested groups. Eventually, in August 1994, I became a Reiki Master, the term applied to teachers of this healing art. That was a profound and moving spiritual experience beyond anything I had previously known, not only for the incredible visions, personal insight and enlightenment I received during the spiritual empower-ment, but also for the awesome knowledge and responsibility of what I had taken on. I realised immediately that I had taken only my first few steps on a very special spiritual path towards the mastery of Reiki, for being a Reiki Master is a lifelong learning journey with the aim of developing an understanding of this amazing, wonderful, powerful lifeforce energy we call Reiki. At the end of 1995 I took the plunge and gave up my job to become a Reiki Master full-time, teaching Reiki and other mind/body healing techniques to hundreds of people all over Britain.

Reiki has totally transformed my life. I am so much happier, so much more content than I have ever been before, and I believe I am living the life I was meant to live, following the path that feels right for me. Although the changes occurred slowly and gently, my life now has a balance, more order, harmony and stability than there used to be. Now I recognise that Reiki has flowed into all areas of my life: into my relationships, into the way I work, into my dreams, ambitions and goals, even into the way I eat. It is there in my hands whenever I want it to be, and it has led me to many interesting experiences, taught me so much and helped me so much. Through Reiki I have met hundreds of lovely people, and it has been a pleasure and a privilege to help so many to experience the joy and wonder of those first moments when the Reiki flows through their hands. Teaching Reiki is the most satisfying job I've ever had, not least because I realise that I am helping people to achieve their potential, moving them on to the next stage of their life path. It's also a lot of fun!

You cannot learn Reiki from this or any other book. This ability can only be acquired by participating in an attunement process (see Chapter 1), which is a form of spiritual empowerment whereby a Reiki Master conveys this skill to you by opening your inner healing channel to allow the Reiki to flow through you. The aim of this book is to provide a comprehensive and accessible introduction to the subject of Reiki, where it came from, how it works and what it can achieve. I have also outlined what the training process involves, as well as giving details of how to find a practitioner and an appropriate course. In addition, there are some visualisation exercises and ideas for activities which may be both useful and good fun, as well as a list of other books on various metaphysical topics that may help you in your search for spiritual awareness and growth.

My personal belief is that there are many paths to the truth, and that Reiki is one of those paths. I also believe that when the time is right and you have reached a particular stage in your own personal path of spiritual development, Reiki starts to send out messages to you and it begins to turn up in your life. Reiki finds you, rather than you finding Reiki. I wish you much joy in your life with Reiki.

Penelope Quest

1

What is Reiki?

The word 'Reiki' is Japanese, and it means 'universal life-force energy'. In the late 19th century a Japanese priest, Dr Mikao Usui, rediscovered a way of channelling this healing energy, creating the Usui System of Natural Healing, or Usui Shiki Ryoho, which has become better known simply as 'Reiki'.

Reiki is a totally safe, non-intrusive hands-on healing technique for physical ailments, but it is much more than a physical therapy. It is an holistic system for healing body, mind, emotions and spirit, and it can also be used to encourage personal and spiritual awareness and growth.

The Meaning of the Word 'Reiki'

In the Japanese alphabet (Kanji), Reiki is really composed of two words – 'Rei' and 'Ki' (pronounced RAY–KEE). There are a number of potential variations, but it is possible to summarise the meanings thus:

☆ 'Rei' is the Higher Intelligence that guides the creation

REI	Universal, Boundless, Transcendental Spirit, Soul, Divine, Sacred, Essence, Mysterious Power, God's Wisdom, Higher Power, Supernatural Knowledge, Spiritual Consciousness
KI	Lifeforce Energy, Cosmic Energy, (also known as Chi, Qi, Prana, Mana, Light, Holy Ghost, Bioplasmic Energy)

Japanese pictogram for Reiki

and functioning of the universe, the wisdom that comes from God (or the Source, the Creator, the Universe or All That Is) which is all knowing and understands the need for and cause of all problems and difficulties and how to heal them.

☆ 'Ki' is the lifeforce energy that flows through every living thing – plants, animals and people.

When these words are put together, therefore, the meaning of 'Reiki' is simplified as 'universal lifeforce energy', or 'God-directed lifeforce energy' – energy guided by a subtle wisdom to balance, heal and harmonise all aspects of the person, body, mind, emotions and spirit.

What is Healing?

The dictionary definition of the word 'healing' is to restore or be restored to health. Most people seem to think of healing as something which happens 'out there', that healing is carried out by someone else, whether that other person is a doctor, a therapist, or a practitioner of a complementary therapy. But there is only one 'healer' in your life – *you*.

Consider what happens when you cut yourself. The cut doesn't continue to bleed, or remain open for the rest of your life. It heals, doesn't it? So who heals it? *You do*. Your body possesses all the healing power it needs, and that healing is activated when something goes wrong. Think of every time you've had a cold. No matter what medications you took, from a simple aspirin to one of the more complex preparations that seek to reduce your symptoms for at least 12 hours, there is no known 'cure' for a cold. It is a virus which has defeated scientists for many years. But your body disposes of it. Your immune system is mobilised, and usually within a few days you are feeling healthy again. Indeed, it is your body's reaction to the virus which gives you all of those nasty symptoms, such as a runny nose and a tickly cough.

You may question this assumption of being able to heal yourself when you consider serious illnesses such as cancer, but there are many reported cases of people who have healed themselves, sometimes with astonishing speed. However, they have usually used a variety of techniques to help them to activate their own healing ability, because the causes of any serious condition are likely to be complex and multi-levelled. Healing is a very personal process. Though many people think of it as occurring at a physical level, the reality is much wider, encompassing mind, emotions and spirit as well as the physical body.

Illness as a Message From Your Body

More and more people involved in health care now believe that treating the physical body without healing the other aspects of the self – the mental, emotional, and spiritual – is like putting a sticky plaster on a burst tyre. It might help for a while, but it should be viewed as a temporary solution while you identify and deal with the cause. Otherwise the problem will occur again, either in the same form or as some new disease, until the message your body is telling you is heeded and you have a change in consciousness.

The body isn't simply a machine or a collection of chemicals, but a conscious energy system. When the body develops any form of illness, it is trying to bring something to your attention. The message may be that something isn't right in your life, or you are going in the wrong direction, or that you are ignoring lessons to be learned. Many people pay no attention to this body language, not because they don't want to, but because they are simply unaware of it. Most people react to sickness by trying to get rid of the symptoms as quickly as possible with medical intervention. There is nothing wrong in seeking relief for symptoms, but if you want your body to be healed you also need to understand *why* you are ill. Obviously there are physical causes for illness, such as viruses and bacteria, but not everyone exposed to a particular virus or bacterium actually 'catches' the illness. Similarly, not everyone who is exposed to carcinogenic agents develops cancer, nor do all people with a genetic predisposition to a disease suffer from it.

So why do we become ill? Illness or disease is created by the body – and the body is simply a part of our consciousness. In other words, we create our own ill-health. If you are frequently unwell, could the underlying reason (or 'dis-ease') be that you are unhappy or too stressed at work, but the only way you will give yourself permission to take time off is to be ill? Is being sick a way of getting more attention or affectionate responses from your family or partner? Do you 'need' an illness to slow you down because you have reached a stage in your spiritual life when you need lots of time by yourself for inner reflection? The body offers messages for you to examine, understand and then act upon, making necessary changes in your life to bring about harmony and good health.

The Greeks and the Chinese were probably the first to chronicle the link between physical ill-health and mental 'dis-ease' several thousand years ago, but the mind/body connection has been a part of healing theories in almost every civilisation throughout history. The study of psychology and more recently of psycho-neuro-immunology has added to our understanding of the complex links between our mental and emotional state and our physical condition.

The following list shows some of the possible relationships between parts of the body and facets of our inner selves, as a very rough guide:

Left side of body	Represents our feminine side and our inner journey, as well as creativity, imagination, spiritual and psychic issues.
Right side of body	Represents our masculine side and our outer journey, as well as money or job issues, or other practical, physical and material concerns.
Eyes	Show how we 'see' the world. What are you not prepared to see? Are you looking at things from an unhelpful perspective?
Ears	What are you unwilling to hear? Are you avoiding listening to your inner guidance?
Throat	Communication issues. Have you swallowed your anger and hurt? Are you expressing your feelings? Are you telling the truth?
Shoulders	Are you carrying too many burdens? Do you always put yourself last in your list of priorities? Is your life too stressful?
Arms	What or who are you holding on to? Are you afraid to let go? Who or what would you like to embrace?
Hands	Associated with giving (right hand) and receiving (left hand), and the details of life. What issues or situation can't you handle?

Back	Associated with stored anger and resentment, feeling unsupported, and trying to be perfect, as well as money issues and indefinable fears.
Chest (Heart/Lungs)	Relationship issues, self-esteem and feelings of worthlessness, suppressed emotions, feeling smothered or controlled by others.
Legs	Associated with progress through life, fear of change, fear of the future, and family or parental issues. Who/what is holding you back?
Knees	Linked with stubbornness, inflexibility and indecision. What decision are you afraid to make? Are you being obstinate over something?
Ankles	Do you need to change direction? Is your life unbalanced?
Feet	Associated with security and survival, reaching our goals or completing tasks, fear of taking the next step, being 'grounded'.

Such descriptions are only very brief examples of a complex issue. It may sound simplistic to say that, for example, a sore throat may result from problems expressing yourself, but 'healing' in this expanded sense involves the realisation that you have a direct and important role to play in activating your own vibrant health. If we are able to create illness, we can also create health. This is very empowering because it means that you have some choice in the matter. You can choose to help yourself in lots of different ways, from adopting a healthier diet and lifestyle, to deciding what sort of healing needs to take place and mobilising your creative forces to bring this about. Reiki can be a valuable and powerful tool in this process. Not only does it help to alleviate physical symptoms, but it encourages understanding of the causes of your physical 'dis-ease', whether mental, emotional or spiritual, and it supports whatever healing programme you undertake.

It is important to understand, however, that 'healing' is not always the same as 'curing', although we tend to use the

words interchangeably. Curing means to completely eradi-
cate the illness or disease, whereas healing can occur on
many different levels:

☆ Healing on the physical level, which could mean eradicat-
ing the illness, or might simply mean limiting or alleviating
the symptoms for a time;

☆ Healing on the emotional level, allowing you to calm any
fears and to reach an acceptance of the effects of the illness;

☆ Healing on the mental level, bringing to your attention
the lessons your illness is trying to teach you, and promoting
understanding of the causative issues;

☆ Healing on the spiritual level, allowing you to love yourself unconditionally, or perhaps even to make a peaceful
transition into death.

The potential for multi-level healing with Reiki is unlimited.
It may be uncomfortable to accept, but we place limits on
our own healing by what we believe is or is not possible. For
instance, we know that a cold will last only three or four
days, and a broken leg is usually mended in about six weeks,
but we anticipate that serious or chronic illnesses such as
cancer or arthritis are either difficult or impossible to cure.
From the metaphysical point of view this mindset inhibits our
own healing potential. If we think something can't be cured,
it probably won't be! Conversely, if we believe we can get
better, our chances of doing so are very much improved. It is
vital to 'think positively'. A considerable body of medical
research now confirms this. Dr Bernie Siegel, in his book
Love, Medicine and Miracles gives many examples, including a

discovery by a group of researchers in London. They found that the ten-year survival rate for cancer patients who reacted to their diagnosis with a 'fighting spirit' was 75 per cent, compared to only 22 per cent in those who responded with hopelessness or resignation.

How Reiki Healing Works

Our whole energy field, including our physical body, is responsive to thoughts and feelings, and the flow of energy becomes disrupted or blocked whenever we accept or acknowledge negative thoughts or feelings about ourselves, whether this is done consciously or unconsciously (see Chapter 2). Reiki helps to break through these blockages, flowing through the affected parts of the energy body and the aura, charging them with positive energy and raising the vibratory level of the whole energy field. It clears and balances the chakras and straightens the energy pathways (meridians) to allow the lifeforce to flow in a healthy and natural way around the whole body. This accelerates the body's own natural ability to heal physical ailments, and opens the mind to an acceptance and understanding of the body's messages about the causative issues which have led to 'dis-ease' in both our physical and energy bodies. Because Reiki is guided by a Higher Intelligence, it always finds its way to those areas of the physical body and the energy body most in need of healing, without any conscious direction from either the healer or the person being healed. It adjusts to suit the recipient, so that each person receives as much or as little healing as they need.

However it is important not to have fixed expectations about the outcome of receiving Reiki. Because Reiki works holistically, it will flow through you to unblock the causative level of 'dis-ease'. While your conscious mind might think help with a physical symptom is the priority, your sub-conscious, or higher self, will identify the underlying metaphysical causes, whether emotional, mental or spiritual, so healing may need to take place on those levels first. You don't even need to believe in Reiki for it to work – it works on animals, and they don't know what it is! No conscious effort on your part is necessary; if you are willing to receive the Reiki, healing *will* take place, although it might work in unexpected ways!

Ultimately if you want the healing to be permanent you have to take responsibility for healing the cause. This may mean changing how you think or the way you relate to other people or even altering your lifestyle, from your home to your kind of career. Surprisingly, perhaps, Reiki can help with these adjustments too, allowing you to approach the changes in a calm, relaxed state of mind.

Reiki is not a religion, but a healing connection to the universal lifeforce, so it is available to, and appropriate for, anyone of any religious or spiritual background. You need no particular beliefs in order to learn or use Reiki, and no complicated rituals are required.

The ability to channel Reiki can only be acquired when it is transferred to the student by a Reiki Master, during the special attunement process that forms part of a Reiki course or seminar. This attunement process makes Reiki unique, and is one of the major differences between Reiki and other methods of hands-on healing, such as spiritual healing. It is also the reason why the ability to heal can be developed so quickly yet so permanently. From the time you receive the Reiki attunement you are able to call upon this universal life-force energy at any time, in any place, for as long as you live. The ability to channel Reiki doesn't wear off or wear out.

Even if you stop using it, Reiki will still be available to you years later, although you may need to practise a little to re-establish the same quantity of flow.

The attunement process creates a Reiki channel – perhaps the closest analogy would be a spiritual equivalent to a fibre-optic tube – through which Reiki (and *only* Reiki) can flow. Then, whenever you intend to use Reiki, simply thinking about it or holding your hands out in readiness to use it will activate it. This universal lifeforce energy will then be drawn in through the Crown chakra, and from there it will flow down the Reiki channel, through the Brow, Throat and Heart chakras, and then down each arm, eventually streaming out of the Palm chakras. Some people report 'seeing' the Reiki energy as a vortex of energy (usually as a double helix, similar to DNA) pouring into the Crown chakra of the practitioner, and then out of each hand.

The Reiki flows through this pure channel, and it is *pulled* by the recipient, rather than *pushed* by the practitioner, although this is not a conscious process, because it is controlled by the recipient's higher self, so the recipient doesn't need to do anything. It is not the healer's own energy, but comes directly from the Higher Intelligence, flowing through a pure channel, so it cannot be affected by the way the practitioner feels. This means that the person receiving the Reiki cannot pick up any negativity from the practitioner. The energy can only flow in one direction so it also means that the practitioner cannot pick up any negativity from the client through the Reiki channel. Both practitioner and client are totally protected during the treatment.

When Reiki is used in this way, the majority of the flow comes out of the hands to be used either for self-treatment or for other people, plants or animals. However, some Reiki flows out of the Heart chakra into and around the healer's

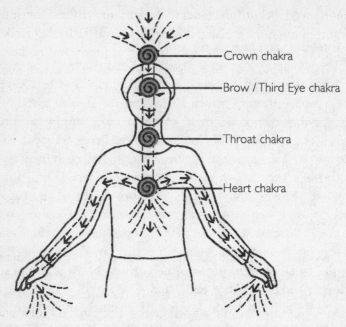

Crown chakra

Brow / Third Eye chakra

Throat chakra

Heart chakra

The flow of Reiki energy

own energy body. This is one of the reasons why Reiki practitioners don't become tired when doing Reiki treatments on other people. They usually feel energised, because they have also been receiving some Reiki.

The Effects Of Reiki

People's experiences of Reiki are very varied, although there are some common themes. When Reiki is flowing through their hands, or when receiving Reiki from a practitioner, people feel a range of sensations, from gentle tingling or a sense of inner vibration, to heat or even coldness. Some people have little or no sensation, but this does not indicate any lack of effectiveness. They sometimes report having experienced beautiful colours, dreams or visions, or long forgotten memories arising during or soon after having Reiki, and most describe a wonderful feeling of peace and radiance afterwards. However, it isn't necessary to experience such distinctive sensations to enjoy the benefits of Reiki. Most people achieve a deep state of relaxation which allows physical, mental or emotional stress to leave the body, re-establishing equilibrium and a feeling of well-being.

Reiki can transform your life in many powerful and wonderful ways. It balances and works on four levels of existence, and adjusts itself to the recipient so that each person receives exactly what they need:

☆ **Physical** The physical body and any pain or illness. Reiki supports and accelerates your body's own natural ability to heal itself, helping to alleviate pain and relieve other symptoms while cleansing the body of poisons and toxins. Reiki balances and harmonises the whole energy body, promoting a sense of wholeness, a state of positive wellness and an overall feeling of well-being. It also helps you to develop a greater awareness of your body's real needs.

☆ **Emotional** What you are feeling and experiencing. Reiki encourages you to examine your emotional responses, encouraging you to let go of negative emotions and promoting the qualities of loving, caring, sharing, trusting and good will. It also helps you to channel emotional energy into creativity.

☆ **Mental** Your thoughts and attitudes. Reiki leads to a state of deep relaxation, with the consequent release of stress and tension. It allows you to let go of negative thoughts, concepts and attitudes, replacing them with positivity, peace and serenity. It also enhances your intuitive abilities and encourages you to pursue your personal potential through greater insight and self-awareness.

☆ **Spiritual** Your capacity to love yourself and others unconditionally. Reiki helps you to accept and love your whole self, and fosters a non-judgemental approach to humankind, allowing you to accept every person as a soul energy as well as a human being. It promotes the qualities of love, compassion, understanding and acceptance, and encourages you on your personal path towards spiritual development and connectedness with the Divine.

2

Understanding
Subtle Energies

The subtle energy fields that permeate and surround our bodies are integral to our health and well-being.

The Human Energy Field

Science now confirms what spiritual traditions throughout the ages have always known — that everything in the universe is connected. Everything is composed of energy or light vibrating at different rates so that the denser, solid objects are oscillating at a slower rate than less tangible, 'invisible' elements. Your physical body is made of energy vibrating at a relatively slow rate, making it solid, whereas the layers of your auric field, or energy body, vibrate at higher frequencies. These are harder to see with the naked eye, but can now be detected by scientific instruments, and even photographed using the specially developed Kirlian camera.

The knowledge that an unseen energy flows through all living things and is connected directly to the quality of health has been part of the wisdom of many cultures for thousands of years. All living creatures have energy bodies, as do what we might term 'inanimate' objects such as rocks, crystals and water. The energy which comprises the human energy field has various names, depending upon the culture or spiritual tradition – the lifeforce; ki (Japanese); chi or qi (Chinese); the Light or the Holy Ghost (Christian); or prana (Indian). It is composed of an external field known as the aura, energy centres known as chakras, and a range of energy channels flowing through the body called meridians.

The Aura

The aura is a field of light or energy that completely surrounds the physical body, above, below and on all sides. It can be detected by dowsing with rods or pendulums, and it

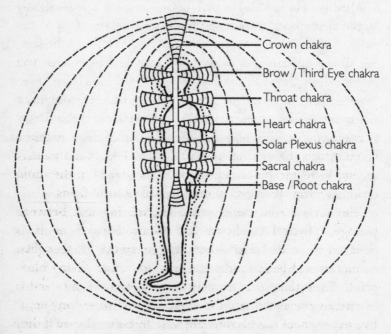

The seven auric layers and seven chakras

can also be sensed or felt with the hands. Some people are able to see it, reporting layers of soft colour, particularly around the head and shoulders. Seeing auras can take practice, but you can experiment with the simple instructions on page 22.

The human aura has seven layers. The inner layers, closest to the physical body, are the densest, and each succeeding layer is composed of finer and higher vibrations. The outer layers are often 15–30 feet (5–10 metres) or more away from the physical body. The aura is not always the same size. It can expand or contract depending upon a variety of factors including your state of health, your current emotional and mental condition, or your sense of being comfortable with the people in your immediate surroundings.

Most people have an oval (elliptical) aura which is slightly larger at the back than at the front and fairly narrow at the sides. Although we may not be consciously aware of the fact, we all use our auras as valuable sensing devices – what you might call the 'eyes in the back of your head'. Have you ever experienced that strange 'prickle' at the back of your neck when someone has been looking at you from behind? Or perhaps you've been able to sense the atmosphere within a room before you've even opened the door? As your aura may extend 5–10 metres ahead of you, it is already in the room picking up the vibrations of other people's auric fields.

The aura is sometimes called the missing link between biology, physical medicine and psychotherapy, as it is believed to be the place where all our emotions, thoughts, memories and behaviour patterns begin – our 'living blueprint'. Everything that happens to us affects the aura and is eventually translated into the physical body, where any negative experiences can become physical illness or disease if they are not cleared and healed.

EXERCISE: SEEING AURAS

Seeing Your Own Aura

To see your own aura it is easiest to look at either (or both) of your hands. Hold your hand out at arm's length, with the fingers spread wide apart, preferably against a plain background. Some people find it easiest with a light background, while others prefer something dark, so you need to experiment. You are looking for a faint outline close to and surrounding the fingers. It usually appears as lighter than the colour of your finger, although sometimes it is seen as a slightly darker smudgy line.

It's important to feel relaxed about this. A soft gaze is much more likely to achieve results than a fiercely concentrated stare, and it is easier to do in daylight rather than artificial light. Don't expect to see masses of coloured light, as shown in a Kirlian photograph. The auric field is usually softly coloured, but it is very subtle, and is often sensed rather than seen, so don't be disheartened if all you see is a soft pale glow.

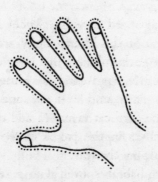

A hand showing an energy field

Seeing Other Auras

When you've successfully detected the aura around your own fingers, you might like to look for other people's auric fields. It is unusual to see auras all the time; most people 'switch on' this ability by actively looking, so you're unlikely to notice them while wheeling your trolley around the supermarket! It is simplest when a person is involved in something important to them, such as giving an impassioned speech, because the aura seems to intensify at such times. It can be seen as a soft white or golden glow surrounding their head and shoulders, growing larger as they become more involved in their subject. Again, it will probably be best if they have a plain background behind them, but the more you practise 'active looking' the easier it becomes. Eventually you will probably begin to see (or sense) shades of other colours.

Animals and plants have auras, too, so there's no end to the fun once you've developed the technique of seeing subtle energy fields.

The Chakras

Chakra is a Sanskrit word meaning wheel or vortex. The seven major chakras in the human body are shown in the diagram on page 20, each linked to one layer of the aura. The Base chakra is linked to the auric layer closest to the body, the Sacral chakra to the second layer out, and so on up to the Crown chakra at the furthest layer. In addition we have 21 minor chakras, such as in the palms of the hands, on the knees and on the soles of the feet.

A healthy chakra vibrates evenly in a circular motion, resembling a funnel that is fairly narrow close to the body but becoming wider as it gets further out. These are detectable using a pendulum held over the chakra point. The outer edge of the chakra may be only a few inches from the body or several feet away, depending upon our physical, mental and emotional state.

The chakras are intimately connected with our physical health. Each is linked with specific parts of the body and to systems within the body. When a particular chakra is healthy, balanced and open, so are its connected body parts, but if a chakra is blocked, damaged or closed, then the health of the connected body parts and systems begins to reflect this. Our chakras are affected by everything which happens to us, good things as well as bad. For example, falling in love has an amazingly beneficial effect on our whole energy body, whereas emotional or mental traumas and even negative words can have detrimental effects on the energy levels.

Whenever problems are not dealt with, negative energy can build up and remain within the energy field of the chakra for a long time, 'blocking' the correct flow of energy and distorting its shape. For example, if someone often has difficulty in talking about their true feelings, a block may begin to build up in the fifth chakra, located at the throat. Alternatively, they may have serious problems with money or their job, so blockages might occur in the Root chakra, located at the base of the spine. If the person deals with the problems by facing up to them and finding solutions, then the blocked energy will disperse. If not the blockages can build up until the chakra becomes deformed and minor illnesses can then occur in the associated body parts or systems. These illnesses are 'messages' from the body and are intended to help us to identify what is wrong in our lives so that we have an opportunity to put things right. If we ignore the lesson our body is trying to teach us, or are simply unaware that the illness is a message, then the chakra could even become completely closed. At that stage serious illness or disease is almost inevitable.

The chart below shows the locations of each chakra, together with its associated colour, body parts and systems, and associated life aspects.

The Chakra System

Number/ Chakra	Location	Colour	Body Parts/ Systems	Associated Life Aspects
Seventh Chakra Crown	top of head	purple or violet	Pineal, nervous system, brain, whole body.	Knowledge, spirituality, understanding, unity, connection, universal consciousness. *I Know*
Sixth Chakra Brow/ Third Eye	centre of forehead	indigo	Pituitary, hypothalamus, endocrine system, head, eyes, face.	Clairvoyance, intuition, imagination, spiritual awareness, individual consciousness. *I See*
Fifth Chakra Throat	throat	blue	Thyroid, parathyroid, growth, metabolism, ears, nose, mouth, teeth, neck, throat.	Communication, expression, creativity, abundance, receiving. *I Speak*
Fourth Chakra Heart	centre of chest (sternum)	green (or pink)	Thymus, respiration, circulation, immune system, heart, lungs, upper back, arms, hands.	Unconditional love, balance, unity, relationships, affinity, giving, acceptance. *I Love*
Third Chakra Solar Plexus	solar plexus	yellow	Pancreas, muscles, digestive system, liver, gall bladder, middle back.	Personal power, will, control, self-definition, energy, intellect. *I Can*
Second Chakra Sacral	abdomen (navel)	orange	Testes/ovaries, reproduction system, kidneys, uterus, lower digestive organs, lower back.	Emotions, sensations, sexuality, food, appetite, movement, pleasure. *I Feel*
First Chakra Root/ Base	base of spine	red	Adrenals, skeleton, skin, elimination system, senses, pelvis, hips, legs, feet.	Survival, security, trust, grounding, physical body, money, home, job. *I Have*

Your aura and chakras regulate themselves quite naturally throughout your life. When you develop awareness of them you can help yourself by carrying out a visualisation, such as the one at the end of this chapter, that will help to cleanse and strengthen your aura and balance, clear and harmonise your chakras.

Healing Energies

When you feel happy, healthy and balanced, your whole energy body will be 'sparkly'. When you feel sad, angry or confused your energy body is dull. Equally, when your ki, or lifeforce, is high and flowing freely, you feel healthy, strong, confident, full of energy, ready to enjoy life and take on its challenges, and you are much less likely to become ill. If your ki is low, or there is a restriction or blockage in its flow, you feel weak, tired and lethargic, and are much more vulnerable to illness or 'dis-ease'.

Ki is all around us. We naturally absorb it every day through our auric fields and by breathing it into our physical bodies. It is a vital part of our inherent healing ability, as it helps to nourish the structure, organs and systems of the body, supporting them in their vital functions and contributing to the healthy growth and renewal of cells. The amount we absorb is not constant and can depend on many factors, and we do not always sufficiently replenish our supply of ki through natural means.

Normal healthy young children usually take in as much ki as they need naturally. You only have to watch them to see that their energy levels are high! People who study ancient spiritual practices, special breathing techniques or martial arts are also often able to focus additional energy and draw ki into their bodies. However the rest of us may not draw in as much energy as we need, particularly as we get older, because our aura and chakras become increasingly blocked or damaged, and we often develop the habit of shallow breathing, so that our reserves become depleted. You may have experienced this yourself in specific instances. If you have spent time with a friend going through some emotionally traumatic event, after a few hours of talking supportively to them, you may begin to feel drained and tired. This is because you have 'donated' your lifeforce energy, or have allowed it to be drawn off into your friend's energy field.

This is one way in which we can 'heal' using our own lifeforce energy for the benefit of others. Other examples include cuddling a child to stop it crying, or placing a hand on a cut or painful part of the body. At this level, we may not think of ourselves as 'healers', but we are helping our own or another person's healing process by using our personal supply of ki energy. Lifeforce energy flows into and out of the chakras more easily than through other parts of the body, which is one reason why 'hands-on healing' is successful, as it is easy for energy to flow out through the Palm chakra.

Hands-on healing has been used for many thousands of years in virtually every religion, culture and society. Some healers use their own lifeforce energy to heal others, but they can easily become exhausted if they use too much, because the body needs sufficient time to replenish its energy supply. Other spiritual healers help to focus the energies supplied by 'unseen friends' – people on the spiritual realm who have agreed to help humanity in this way. Some are able to draw into themselves healing energy from the Source which then flows into the person they are healing.

Reiki healing is similar to this latter form of spiritual healing, although the spiritual healers who have attended my Reiki courses tell me that the two energies 'feel' different as they use them and that Reiki seems to flow instantaneously, unlike other healing energies that build up more slowly. I believe that various strands of healing energy come from the same source, and have different vibrationary frequencies and special purposes. The Chinese healing tradition has a 4,000-year-old text called *The Yellow Emperor's Classic of Internal Medicine* which states that there are 32 different kinds of chi (ki).

To bring it into context, the difference between ki (life-force energy) and Reiki (universal lifeforce energy) is that:

☆ Ki is the energy which surrounds and permeates everything;

☆ Reiki is a specific band or frequency of healing energy which comes directly from the Source (or God, the Creator, All That Is) and is directed by that Higher Intelligence for healing (or wholing) any living thing.

Reiki, like most 'complementary' therapies, works on the energy body, rather than purely on the physical body. Your physical body is really just one component of your wider energy body, or spirit, and that is why it needs to be treated holistically, or 'as a whole'. If your ki, or energy body, is low or blocked or damaged, receiving Reiki replenishes the lost energy reserves and unblocks and repairs the energy body.

EXERCISE: VISUALISATION TO CLEANSE THE AURA AND BALANCE THE CHAKRAS

Visualisations are forms of guided meditation that allow you to access your inner wisdom to gain insight into particular situations which may be affecting you, or that allow you to use your own powerful thought energy to create new conditions in your life. The following visualisation, called 'Bringing In The Light', is designed to cleanse and strengthen your aura, and to clear and balance each chakra to allow lifeforce energy to flow more efficiently throughout your whole energy field. Anyone can carry out this visualisation. You don't need to be able to do Reiki, although if you can it will make it even more effective if you bring Reiki as well as light into your body.

Preparing For The Visualisation

You will find it easier to meditate or visualise if you are in a safe, quiet, softly lit environment where disturbances will be as few as possible. You may like to create a special place in your home where you can sit or lie down in comfort. The experience may be enhanced if you can burn some favourite essential oils or incense sticks and perhaps have some gentle music playing softly in the background.

Two great tools to aid meditation are relaxation and breath control. As part of the process of meditation, you might like to develop the habit of relaxing your body by visualising and feeling it relax, and becoming aware of your breath is a vital stage in the awareness of the body. We normally have no particular perception of breathing. It is simply something we take for granted.

The Relaxation Process

☆ First, sit or lie comfortably, and concentrate for a few minutes on your breathing. Take in a few slow, deep breaths, and allow your breathing to regulate at this slower rate, feeling the breath going deeply into the whole of your lungs.

☆ Now turn your attention to your body, and become aware of your feet. Tense all the muscles in your toes, feet and ankles, and then let them relax completely.

☆ Next tense the muscles of your calves, knees and thighs as tightly as you can, and then let them relax.

☆ Then tense the muscles of your hips, abdomen and chest, and let them relax.

☆ Next tense and then relax the muscles of your shoulders, arms, hands and fingers.

☆ Finally tense your neck, jaw, face and scalp really tight, and then allow all those muscles to lose that tension and relax completely.

☆ If any parts of your body still don't feel totally relaxed, tense them again, and then slowly let the tension out until they feel soft and languid.

Breathing

☆ Breathe in for a count of one, then hold your breath for a count of one, then breathe out for a count of one; repeat this for a count of two, then three, four, five, six, seven, eight and finally nine. Then return to a regular rhythm of breathing.

The Visualisation Process

If you haven't tried visualisations before, don't feel daunted by the prospect of the process. We are all used to imagining things, or daydreaming, or remembering things. That's all that visualising is – using your imagination to take you on a journey in your mind. If you are not a particularly visual person then you may just sense what is happening instead, and that is fine. Some people see only a few dissociated images, or find they complete only part of the visualisation, but you can always return to a visualisation at another time. Gradually the fuller picture will develop. Just like painting, visualising takes practice. Not everyone is a Leonardo da Vinci to begin with!

Part of this visualisation takes you through a rainbow of light to open, clear and balance each chakra. Because each chakra vibrates to a specific colour (as given in the chart on page 25), visualising colour or even wearing clothes of the linked colour, can be helpful in re-establishing balance. Don't worry if you 'see' only some of the colours, or none at all. Not 'seeing' the images doesn't negate the effectiveness of the visualisation, because your subconscious or higher self – that part of you which guides, protects, and knows all about you – will be actively taking part in the visualisation. This means that although it may be pleasant to be consciously aware of what is going on, it isn't strictly necessary. You will benefit anyway, even if you fall asleep!

This particular visualisation is relatively simple. For more complex ones you may find it helpful to record them on to a cassette, speaking slowly and evenly, so that you can then play the tape whenever you want to relax.

'Bringing in the Light'

☆ Sit in a comfortable position and allow your body to relax. Begin to be aware of your breathing, and follow your breath in and out ... in and out ... and with each breath you are becoming more and more relaxed. Now imagine that you are breathing in beautiful bright white light. See or feel this brilliant white light swirling around, filling your head, and with every inward breath the light flows into more of your body, down into your neck, shoulders, and arms, moving right down into your hands to the very tips of your fingers. Then you see or sense it flowing through your chest and down into your abdomen, and then into your thighs, knees, and down into your calves and ankles and into your feet, right to the tips of your toes. You feel your feet becoming heavier and more solid, and you can feel the connection with the floor beneath you. Then allow the white light to flow out of your feet into the earth. Imagine the white light forming roots growing from your feet down into the earth, anchoring you and making you feel very secure.

☆ Now that the whole of your body is flooded with white light, you can use this light to form a protective barrier around you. Imagine that the light is coming out of your hands. Visualise yourself moving your hands over all of your body, so that a cloak of white light surrounds you until the whole of your aura is filled with white light. Allow that light to spread out even further, filling the room. Watch the light swirl into all the corners, from floor to ceiling, from wall to wall, from door to window, until the whole room is bathed in white light.

☆ Take your attention back to your body. Allow the white light to slowly change colour, until you are breathing in warm red light. Allow this red light to flow down and down your body until it reaches your Root chakra at the base of your spine. Feel the red light clearing and balancing your Root chakra, and then sense it spreading out to fill the lower part of your body. Observe it flowing down your legs and into your feet. You can even see it flowing down into the roots of light you have created into the earth.

☆ With your next breath you see the light changing to vibrant orange, and you allow this light to flow down your body until it reaches your Sacral chakra, near your navel. You feel the orange light clearing and balancing your Sacral chakra, and then spreading out to fill all of that part of your body.

☆ Next allow yourself to breathe in golden yellow light, and see this yellow light flow down your body until it reaches your solar plexus, spreading out to clear and balance your Solar Plexus chakra.

☆ Next the light changes to a lovely soft green, and this green light flows down into your chest, where it clears, balances and harmonises your Heart chakra. As it does so it spreads out to fill the whole of your chest, flowing also down your arms and into your hands, until even your fingers are filled with this lovely green light.

☆ The light then changes to a beautiful bright blue, and this blue light fills your throat and neck, and you see it swirling around, clearing and balancing your Throat chakra.

☆ Your next breath brings in a deeper, indigo light, and this light flows up into your head, swirling around your Brow chakra, and you sense it clearing and balancing your 'third eye'.

☆ Finally you see the light you are inhaling change to a beautiful violet or purple, and this light flows up to the top of your head, where it clears and balances your Crown chakra, and you sense that chakra opening like the petals of a flower, allowing the violet light to stream out, tinting your aura with its delicate rays.

☆ Enjoy the peace and tranquillity of your protected space. Allow any stray thoughts that come into your mind to simply drift across, and remain in a relaxed, meditative state for five or ten minutes, or as long as you feel comfortable.

☆ Whenever you are ready, gently become aware again of your surroundings, stretch your fingers and toes, allow your eyes to open, and feel relaxed, yet refreshed and alert.

3

The Origins of Reiki

No one really knows the true origins of the healing system we call Reiki, but it was certainly in use 2,500 years ago, and it is undoubtedly much older than that. The current system of healing was rediscovered and developed by a Japanese priest called Mikao (or Mikaomi) Usui in the latter part of the 19th century. There are now three versions of the Reiki story. For many years it was an oral history, passed down from master to student by word of mouth. This traditional version came from Hawayo Takata, who brought Reiki out of Japan and who was the only Reiki Master teaching in the West between 1938 and 1973. Following the custom of Eastern Masters, Takata taught by example, using stories to illustrate her teaching, rather than providing the detailed explanations to which we are accustomed in the West. No one questioned the accuracy of her Reiki history until the early 1990s when some Masters, seeking more information about the origins of Reiki, began to carry out research in Japan and America. They found some anomalies and contradictions, but the essential points of the traditional story proved to be correct, although it had become Christianised, perhaps to make it more palatable to Americans after the events of Pearl Harbour.

When I was a student on a Reiki First Degree course in 1991, I was told the traditional history of the way in which Dr Usui rediscovered Reiki. I felt then that it was a beautiful, inspirational story, and I still think so today.

The Traditional Story

Dr Mikao Usui

Dr Mikao Usui was the Principal of Doshisha, a small Christian university in Kyoto in Japan, where he was one day challenged by his students to show them proof of the healing and miracles reported in the Bible. They asked when they were going to be taught how to heal. Being an extremely honourable Japanese gentleman, and recognising that he could not teach his students what they asked of him, he resigned his position to dedicate his life to rediscovering how Jesus healed. He believed that he would be able to discover what he was seeking if he began his quest in a Christian country, so he travelled to America to study at the University of Chicago. Despite receiving a doctorate in theology, he still did not find what he was looking for, so he returned to Japan where he began visiting the Buddhist monasteries, searching for someone who had an interest in, and some knowledge of, physical healing.

Dr Usui talked to many Buddhist priests and scholars, who always answered his questions about physical healing in the same way, telling him that those teachings had been lost long ago, because it was considered more important to heal the spirit than the body. He eventually came across the abbot of a Zen monastery who allowed him to study the sacred writings in the Japanese Lotus Sutras (ancient teachings), and he learned other languages so that he could also study Chinese sacred teachings and the Sanskrit sutras of Tibet. Within these ancient Buddhist sutras he discovered formulae and symbols (see Chapter 6) which seemed to hold the answers to his quest, but although he believed he had the necessary technical information, he was unable to activate the healing ability.

The abbot suggested that he should make a spiritual pilgrimage to the holy mountain of Kurama where he should fast and meditate for 21 days in the hope of receiving the necessary enlightenment. This he did, setting 21 stones in front of him as a way to count the days. On the 21st day, just as the first rays of the sun began to show in the sky, he threw the last stone away and looked towards the horizon, wondering what he should do next.

Suddenly a strong beam of light came towards him at great speed. As it came closer he felt afraid but realised that he had been seeking enlightenment and must accept whatever would come to him. He waited until the powerful light struck him on the forehead, and he lost consciousness. His spirit then rose out of his body, and he was shown beautiful rainbow-coloured bubbles of light, each containing the keys or symbols of Reiki which he had seen in the ancient sutras. As he reflected upon each symbol he received an attunement to that symbol, was given the sacred mantra by which it should be known and acquired knowledge of how to use it. In this way he was initiated into Reiki. He heard a voice saying, 'These are the keys to healing; learn them; do not forget them; and do not allow them to be lost'. Then his spirit returned to his body and he gradually came out of his altered state of consciousness.

Despite having been on retreat for 21 days, he realised that he no longer felt exhausted, stiff or hungry, as he had just before dawn on that last day. Excitedly he began to make his way back down the mountain, and on his journey several things happened to demonstrate that the healing gift he had been seeking really had been granted to him. In his haste he stubbed his toe, and quite naturally bent down to hold his foot in his hands. As he did so, he felt warmth flowing into his toe; the pain and bleeding stopped and his toe appeared to be healing with amazing speed. When he reached the bottom of the mountain, he stopped at a food stall and ordered a meal. The man serving the food could see from Dr Usui's condition that he had probably been on a long fast, and suggested a light repast would be more suitable, but Dr Usui demanded a full breakfast, and went to sit under a tree to wait for it.

Soon the food-seller's daughter brought him his meal. It was obvious that she had been crying, and her face was red and swollen on one side. The girl told him that she had very bad toothache, but unfortunately her father could not afford dental treatment. Remembering how quickly his toe had healed, Usui asked if he might place his hands on her face to see if this would help. She agreed, and in a few minutes the pain was gone and the swelling began to go down, much to her relief and delight. He then tucked into his large meal with no ill effects, despite his long fast. Later that evening Dr Usui returned to the monastery, anxious to tell the abbot about his experiences. He was told that the abbot was in bed suffering from a painful attack of arthritis, so he went to see his old friend and placed his healing hands on his arthritic joints. Within a short time his pain had gone.

Dr Usui returned to Kyoto where he began to do healing work with the beggars there. He did this for seven years, often having spectacular results that enabled the beggars to begin living a normal life. After a time he noticed that some of those he had helped were returning to the streets in much the same condition as he had found them. He was disappointed, and asked them why they had returned to a beggar's life. They replied that the responsibility of living an ordinary life with a job and a wife and family was too hard, so they were returning to the easier way of life they knew.

Dr Usui was dismayed and upset by this, but he finally acknowledged that what the Buddhist priests had told him was true. Spiritual healing was more important than physical healing. Although he had healed the beggars' physical bodies of symptoms, he had ignored their spiritual needs. He had not taught them an appreciation for life or how to live in a new way, and because he had given the healing freely, they did not value it. Again in meditation he received further guidance from the Higher Intelligence about the healing of the spirit through a conscious decision to take responsibility for one's own health and well-being in order for the Reiki healing energies to have lasting results. He was also given the five spiritual principles of Reiki to balance the physical aspect of his healing work:

☆ Just for today, do not anger;

☆ Just for today, do not worry;

☆ Honour your parents, teachers and elders;

☆ Earn your living honestly;

☆ Show gratitude to every living thing.

He then left the beggars and began to teach others how to heal themselves, sharing with them the principles of Reiki to help them to live in harmony with themselves and others. As a Master, Dr Mikao Usui practised and taught Reiki throughout Japan for the remainder of his life, gathering a following of 16 disciples to whom he passed on Reiki via the Master attunement. When his life was drawing to a close in the late 1920s, he asked one of his students, Dr Chujiro Hayashi, a 47-year-old retired naval officer, to be the next Grand Master of Reiki, to preserve the Reiki teachings so that they would not be lost as they had been in the past.

Dr Chujiro Hayashi

Dr Hayashi went on to further develop the Usui System, splitting the teaching into the three degrees (or levels) of Reiki. In the early 1930s he founded a Reiki clinic in Tokyo, where people could come for treatment and to learn Reiki. He also used the detailed knowledge he gained from carrying out many treatments to create the standard hand positions for both self-treatment and the treatment of others.

Dr Hayashi was a very psychic man, and he had received insight that Japan would take part in the Second World War. As a former naval officer he knew that he would be asked to take part, but he could not reconcile being a Reiki Master with having to fight. He also believed that of the 13 Masters he had initiated, all the men would be called up to fight and would be killed, so he asked Hawayo Takata, a Japanese-American woman living in Hawaii, to be the next Grand Master of Reiki. Dr Hayashi told her many things about the war, including its outcome and what she must do for her own protection and for the protection of Reiki – her ultimate responsibility. When all of his affairs were put in order he called his family and all the Reiki Masters together on 10 May 1941, and, recognising Hawayo Takata as his successor in

Reiki, he said goodbye, closed his eyes and allowed his consciousness to leave his body.

Hawayo Takata

Hawayo Takata was born on 24 December 1900 on the island of Kauai, Hawaii, of Japanese parents who had emigrated from Japan to work in the sugar cane fields. She married and had two daughters, but her husband died and she had to work very hard to raise her children alone. Eventually this hard work took its toll upon her health. In 1935, despite her ill-health, she made a visit to see her parents in Japan, but her condition worsened, and she was taken into hospital for the removal of a tumour. As she was being prepared for surgery, Hawayo Takata sensed that the operation was not necessary, and that there was another way. She questioned one of the doctors, and was told of Dr Hayashi's Reiki clinic nearby.

She began to receive daily treatments from several practitioners at a time. The heat from their hands was so strong that she mistakenly thought they must be using some kind of equipment. Hawayo Takata was further impressed because the Reiki practitioners had also been able to sense what was wrong with her; their diagnosis was virtually identical to that of the hospital doctor.

Within four months Hawayo Takata was healed. She was so inspired and so grateful that she asked to be allowed to learn Reiki. Her request was refused, as Hayashi believed that Reiki should remain in Japan. In addition it was only taught to men (as was the Japanese way in most matters then). Being a very determined woman, and realising that she must show a great commitment to Reiki in order to be allowed to learn, she told Dr Hayashi her feelings and her willingness to sell her house in order to stay in Japan as long as was necessary. He eventually agreed to begin her training, and she and her daughters moved in to live with the Hayashi family. In spring 1936 she received the First Degree attunement, and she worked in the clinic every day for a year as an exchange for the privilege of learning Reiki. After a year of working with Dr Hayashi she received Second Degree Reiki, and returned to Hawaii to set up a Reiki clinic there. She was eventually initiated as a Master in 1938, before finally being appointed Grand Master in 1941.

For many years Hawayo Takata was the only Reiki Master in the West, but she realised how many people needed Reiki, so in the 1970s she began to train other Reiki Masters. But she didn't just teach Reiki – she lived it. She recognised that the Western ways of thinking were very different from those of the East. She believed it was necessary to instil the appropriate respect for the value and sacredness of Reiki, which she felt Westerners would not truly appreciate because it can be learned so easily. She therefore established specific charges for each of the three Reiki degrees: Reiki First Degree (Reiki I) at $150, and $500 for Reiki Second Degree (Reiki II). However, she believed that in order to be a Reiki Master a student must commit their life to healing and teaching Reiki. She had sold her home and worked in Hayashi's clinic for a year without pay to learn Reiki. She wanted to find a way in which Westerners could demonstrate a similar level of commitment. She therefore decreed a much larger fee of $10,000 for people wishing to become Reiki Masters, as she believed this would generate the necessary gratitude, respect and recognition of Reiki as a spiritual calling as well as a healing practice, and would go some way to demonstrating its immense value. Despite inflation these fees have remained unchanged since the 1970s, although lower fees are charged by many Masters now. Those early Reiki students and Masters were certainly making a tremendous financial investment to demonstrate their commitment.

The Alternative Stories

Research by an American Reiki Master, William Rand, revealed that Doshisha University had no record of anyone called Mikao Usui, either as a member of staff or as a student. Further investigation revealed that the University of Chicago also had no knowledge of Dr Usui studying there. He concluded that it was probable that Dr Usui had grown up in the Buddhist tradition, inspired by the Buddha's ability to heal physical illness and to pass on these healing skills to his disciples.

It is probably more likely that Usui would have been able to study the sacred teachings if he was himself a Buddhist priest. Certainly, a Tibetan Buddhist healing technique involving an empowerment, or attunement, transmitted from the teacher to the student, is very similar to modern Reiki practices. It may be that in his constant study of the sacred Sutras, Usui found a technique which had long since been discontinued in Japan. In the true spiritual tradition, he received a mystical experience to reactivate the spiritual lineage so that it might once again be passed on.

More research was undertaken in the mid-1990s by Frank Arjava Petter, a Reiki Master, and his wife Chetna, who both live in Japan. They obtained information from a number of sources including Dr Usui's memorial stone at Saihoji temple in the Toyotama district of Tokyo, which they were able to translate. They discovered that Dr Usui, known as Usui Sensei, had founded the Usui Reiki Ryoho Gakkai (Usui Reiki Healing Method Society) which still exists in Japan today.

From the memorial they discovered that Mikaomi Usui was born on 15 August 1864, and died on 9 March 1926. The inscription also confirms that Dr Usui travelled to the West and to China to study, and that he had a very wide span of knowledge, including medicine, psychology and the theology of many religions. It gives further confirmation that he received enlightenment and inspiration about Reiki healing after a 21-day retreat on Mount Kurama, and that he opened a clinic in Tokyo in 1921 where he gave treatments and ran workshops to pass on his knowledge to others. In all he is reported to have taught over 2,000 people in Japan.

The memorial also gives us personal details about Dr Usui. He is described as 'a very warm, simple and humble person' who 'always had a smile on his face', and who was both 'very courageous' and 'very cautious'. The inscription finishes with the words 'May many understand what a great service Dr Usui did to the world'. (The full story and complete translation of the memorial inscription is included in Frank Arjava Petter's book, *Reiki Fire*.)

From this research it would appear that Dr Hayashi was probably one of Dr Usui's disciples and a respected teacher, rather than a 'Grand Master', as there have been five Presidents of the Usui Reiki Ryoho Gakkai since Usui's death.

What is certain is that Reiki would not have reached the West without him passing on his knowledge to Hawayo Takata. For this, we owe him both gratitude and respect. It is through Takata's 22 Masters that Reiki has spread throughout the world. My own lineage is through the American Reiki Master William Rand, who studied with and was attuned by two different Masters, Cherie Prasuhn and Leah Smith.

At the time of Hawayo Takata's death it was uncertain who would take over the title of Grand Master, which she believed she held, as she appears not to have definitely named a successor. Two people were identified as the most likely — Phyllis Lei Furumoto, who is Takata's granddaughter, and Barbara Weber Ray. At the first ever gathering of Reiki Masters in Hawaii in 1982, Phyllis agreed to follow in her grandmother's footsteps, and was elected to this post by the

Dr Mikao Usui
↓
Dr Chujiro Hayashi
↓
Hawayo Takata
↓
Phyllis Lei Furumoto
↙   ↘
Pat Jack   Carrel Ann Farmer
↓   ↓
Cherie A Prasuhn   Leah Smith
↘   ↙
William L Rand
↓
Penelope Quest

The Lineage of Penelope Quest

majority of the masters. Dr Barbara Weber Ray went on to found The Radiance Technique, which is another branch of Reiki. There are now many thousands of Reiki Masters and millions of people who practice Reiki at either First or Second Degree level.

4

The Development of Reiki as a Healing System

The historic first meeting in 1982 allowed Western Reiki Masters to share their experiences for the first time. They discovered that Hawayo Takata had adopted a unique style of teaching, as each had been taught differently. Even the Reiki symbols each had learned varied slightly, so they took some decisions that have had enormous influence on the development of Reiki as a healing system ever since. They began to standardise the system. They agreed on the exact form of each symbol and on various other aspects of how Reiki should be taught, and then in 1983 at a meeting in British Columbia they formed the Reiki Alliance, an organisation of Reiki Masters who recognise Phyllis Lei Furumoto as the Grand Master, and whose purpose is to support each other as teachers of the Usui System of Reiki.

At that time only the Grand Master was allowed to train or initiate new Masters, but there was a growing demand for more, so in 1988 at a gathering of Reiki Masters in

Friedricksburg Phyllis Lei Furumoto announced that any suitably experienced Master could initiate other Masters. This opened up Reiki to the inevitable changes that result from expansion. By the early 1990s the number of Reiki Masters and practitioners had grown tremendously, so the role of Grand Master had also increased. In response to this expansion Phyllis Lei Furumoto made another major decision in April 1992 to share the role of Grand Master with Paul David Mitchell, another of Takata's original 22 Reiki Masters. They created the 'Office of Grand Master' between them, and Paul Mitchell became the Head of the Discipline, responsible for upholding the Usui System, while Phyllis Lei Furumoto continued to be the Spiritual Lineage Bearer, responsible for carrying the energy and essence of Reiki. Between them they spent several years trying to establish exactly what they believed was the correct form of the Usui System of Reiki Healing. Since the mid-1990s they have been actively encouraging both Masters and practitioners to come into alignment with their approved system.

The Traditional Usui System

According to the Office of the Grand Master, there are four aspects of the Usui System — healing practice, personal growth, spiritual discipline and mystic order — that are connected in a constant cycle of development as each person continues to learn and grow through the practice of Reiki.

The Four Aspects

Healing Practice Most people are attracted to Reiki as a healing practice, and usually they think of this as physical healing. Reiki as a healing practice is a hands-on healing technique where universal lifeforce energy is channelled through

Healing
Practice

Mystic Order   Personal Growth

Spiritual
Discipline

The four aspects of the Usui System

the hands of the practitioner firstly for self-treatment, and then for treatment of other people, animals and plants. However, because Reiki works at the causative level of 'disease', it helps to break through the mental and emotional blocks created by events in people's lives, and heals these at a deep level. The Reiki therefore starts a holistic healing process that can occur at any level within the whole person — body, mind, emotions or spirit — helping to move them towards wholeness, health and well-being.

Personal Growth When Reiki flows through a person on a regular basis, deeper levels of blockage are brought to the surface to be healed and then released. In this way the Reiki begins to stimulate personal growth and development. As it slowly breaks down the blockages and barriers created in the mental, emotional and spiritual bodies, it begins a process which enables an individual to become more self-aware, more understanding and more forgiving of themselves. This in turn leads to a greater acceptance of their true self, which eventually leads to self-love and a growth into wholeness. Because Reiki is guided by a Higher Intelligence, this process always works at a pace suited to the individual, so there are no time limits and the effects are different for each person.

Spiritual Discipline The healing practice and personal growth aspects of Reiki lead to a deepening of our spiritual awareness, the realisation of our relationship to All That Is (or God, the Source, the Creator, or any other preferred term for a higher consciousness). This feeling of connectedness to every living thing brings with it a sense of responsibility, a reverence for all life which is the foundation for a personal view of spirituality and a sense of the sacred within yourself. The very act of treating yourself every day with Reiki is itself a spiritual discipline; the meditative quality of self-treatment encourages a sense of peace and tranquillity and a feeling of oneness with everything around you.

Reiki is a spiritual tool as well as a healing practice, and using the Reiki symbols and their mantras (see Chapter 6) for meditation can bring enormous benefits in spiritual growth and development, as well as profound experiences of enlightenment and deep understanding. In many spiritual traditions it is necessary to study and meditate for many years to reach an understanding of the meaning of your own life, yet Reiki awakens our sense of the divine within everyone and everything.

Mystic Order Further knowledge and experience of Reiki brings increased development of insight and an even deeper acceptance of our connection to all consciousness and the mystery of life. We are so used to wanting to be in control of our lives, to plan, to deliberate, that to surrender to the practice of Reiki and the inexplicable but often wonderful changes which this energy creates in our lives is a challenge. But with Reiki running through our lives we can pause to wonder and appreciate the magical nature of healing, which needs no conscious direction, no personal control. There is a mystic beauty in the form of the initiations, the often amazing spiritual experiences which students receive during the attunement procedure.

When mystery and wonder are inherent in our everyday lives, those lives are richer, and this is the legacy of Reiki. It allows us to accept the unexplainable, to trust the indefinable, and to recognise that if life is a mystery, that's all right. We don't have to understand it all. We just have to *be*.

The Nine Elements of Reiki

The Office of the Grand Master has also outlined the nine elements of practice that constitute the Usui System, which they believe should always be present in the teaching and practice of Reiki:

Oral tradition:	The teaching of Reiki requires that the Reiki Master and student should be physically present together for the initiations, the history, and the personal guidance through the forms of self-treatment and treatment of others.
Spiritual lineage:	The spiritual lineage is seen as the embodiment of the essence of the Usui System, and is carried from Dr Usui through Hayashi and Takata to Furumoto.
History:	The traditional story of the rediscovery of Reiki by Dr Usui is told in classes as part of the oral tradition.
Precepts for daily living:	The five spiritual principles of Reiki: Just for today, do not anger; Just for today, do not worry; Honour your parents, teachers and elders; Earn your living honestly; Show gratitude to every living thing.
Form of classes:	Two degrees or levels, together with the Master level, make up the Usui System. There are specific requirements for what must be taught in First Degree and Second Degree classes. A minimum amount of time is required for this teaching, as well as a recommended time span between classes.
Money:	The recommended fees are those originally set by Hawayo Takata: (in US dollars) $150 for Reiki I, $500 for Reiki II and $10,000 for Reiki Master.
Initiation:	The initiation or attunement process is a sacred ritual which,

<table>
<tr><td>when performed by a Master with a student, results in the capacity to channel Reiki. There are four initiations for Reiki I, one for Reiki II and one for Reiki Master.</td></tr>
</table>

Symbols:	Four Reiki symbols, act as energetic keys, when used in conjunction with Reiki, and these are intended to be kept sacred, and are only taught to students of Second Degree and Master level.
Treatment:	Self-treatment is the first priority, before the treatment of others. There are specific forms of 12 hand positions for each – four on the head, four on the front of the body, and four on the back of the body.

Reiki as a Dynamic Healing System

Those of us involved in Reiki know, and have experienced, that Reiki is a force for change, growth and development in all the people it touches, whether as a client, practitioner or Master. This is also true for Reiki itself. Since Dr Usui re-discovered Reiki it has evolved into the traditional form of practice described here, and it is continuing to evolve.

Phyllis Lei Furumoto is trying to standardise the whole practice of Reiki because she believes that it should be preserved in its current form. She has even attempted to trademark Reiki worldwide in a bid to bring the system under strict control, although her attempts have been unsuccessful in a number of countries, including Britain. Reiki Alliance Masters do indeed follow the official system, but most of the Masters teaching Reiki throughout the world today are independent. In many cases they are trying to expand and individualise the system, and some have devised 'new' systems, channelling different strands of healing energy. Karuna Reiki™ and Tera-Mai™ Seichem are two examples. There are also variations of teaching style and content, some features of which are given in Chapter 6.

I was trained in both the traditional and non-traditional systems, but I actually prefer to teach Reiki in a very traditional way, because I love the true simplicity and gentleness of the process. I find it to be a very beautiful spiritual experience for me, as well as for my students. However, occasionally I have felt drawn to use the 'new' methods, and have found them to be effective and to produce equally special, but different, experiences for those students.

I believe there is a dignity and integrity in the traditional Usui System, but the quality of Reiki Masters is not determined by the price they pay, nor even by the amount of time they spend in training with other Masters. Each Master is on their own personal spiritual journey, and brings a unique lifetime of experience to their interpretation of Reiki. This uniqueness is one of the system's greatest strengths. I have enormous faith in Reiki, and believe implicitly that Reiki will attract those who need it, and will call those who are needed. I also understand that innovation is often threatening, simply because it challenges the status quo.

Reiki is Reiki, whoever needs it, whoever uses it, whoever teaches it. It is a very powerful healing energy directed by a Higher Consciousness, and as such it is unlikely to be kept within the confines of any particular system, however good that system is. We are not in control of it, nor can we ever be. The spirit of Reiki is not open to prescription. It cannot be imprisoned within a set of rules and regulations; it is universal, open, flexible, and flows regardless of the level of personal or spiritual development of the person who channels it.

There are times when I question the advisability of some of the changes, as it is hard to be non-judgemental all the time! But I trust Reiki, and know in my heart that there must be a reason, even if I cannot understand it. What we have to remember is that through it all Reiki works! There is a great need for healing and balance and harmony in the world today. Reiki is perhaps the most important tool available for the raising of consciousness in the next millennium. I have no doubt at all that we shall see further changes and even greater expansion in the next century. I look forward with interest to the new challenges those changes will bring.

5

The Precepts
and Principles
of Reiki

Reiki Precepts

In Dr Usui's many years of healing practice he was convinced of the importance of two things: the necessity for energy exchange if people are to value what they are given; and the need for a change in consciousness for healing to be truly effective and long-lasting.

The Need For Energy Exchange

Many people feel that healing should be given freely, that it is a gift from God which therefore makes it unacceptable to charge for it. What Dr Usui found with the beggars of Kyoto, and what Hawayo Takata believed was particularly true of people in the West, is that we don't seem to value what we don't pay for, and indeed, that we value highly what seems to be expensive. 'You get what you pay for' is the materialistic view.

Healing intrinsically *is* freely given. Reiki energy flows regardless of any financial reward, but it is acceptable, and even necessary, to charge money for Reiki treatments. The practitioner is entitled to make a reasonable living, and he or she is giving their time – a full Reiki treatment takes at least an hour. That time has a value, and should be paid for. I usually suggest to the practitioners I have trained that they should charge roughly the same as an aromatherapy or reflexology treatment.

But money is not the only form of exchange. Close friends and family normally operate a constant and ready exchange all the time, so things naturally even out, given time. With clients it is occasionally more appropriate to accept goods or services in exchange for a treatment – I've been given paintings, books and flowers by people who had very little money, and I've frequently 'swapped' treatments with other practitioners. Many practitioners belong to 'LETS' schemes, where people exchange their skills for a form of local currency, which they can then 'spend' on services or goods from other members.

The principle is that we should value ourselves, and that learning to accept money or gifts in exchange for Reiki is a part of that valuing. Many people find it easier to give than to receive, so there is a meaningful lesson in setting charges for Reiki treatments. Asking for money can feel a bit strange to start with, but it forms an important step in establishing self-worth ... and you will get used to it!

Another aspect of exchange is that by giving continually, you put other people under some form of obligation. Most of us have a well-developed sense of fairness, and it can make us feel uncomfortable if we are always on the receiving end of someone's altruism. Sometimes when healing is given freely people will take advantage of the healer, calling on their services constantly and expecting to be treated at almost any time regardless of the healer's other commitments. Essentially this means they have 'dumped' the problem on the healer and are avoiding taking responsibility for their own healing. Paying money for a treatment, even if it's only a small amount, fosters a sense of involvement in, and commitment to, taking part in their own healing.

Of course I'm not advocating that healing cannot be given for free. I've given Reiki freely many times, in the case of accidents or emergencies, with friends and family, or in demonstrations of Reiki. However when a person makes an appointment for a full treatment they expect me to give them an hour or more of my time, so I charge them accordingly. If I was working at any other job for an hour I would expect to be paid. The same principle applies to teaching Reiki. A Reiki Master is entitled to earn a living, and gives time, energy and experience as well as the incredible gift of Reiki, to every class. What each Master charges is a personal decision based on their own set of values and beliefs about money and about Reiki, rather than on market forces or competition.

The Need For a Change in Consciousness

Whether we take a conventional or a metaphysical view, any illness, pain or disease is a signal from the body that something is wrong. From the conventional viewpoint the indications are fairly basic. If we have a pain in the stomach area then a doctor will look for physical reasons, such as an ulcer, a viral infection or maybe even a grumbling appendix, and will prescribe appropriate treatment which could range from antibiotics to surgery.

From the metaphysical point of view, the message is seen at the causative level, so a stomach pain might indicate that something is happening in your life which you are, literally, finding 'hard to stomach'. Reiki usually alleviates such physical symptoms quite quickly, and because it also works at the causative level, it helps to raise to the surface the issues at the root of the physical problem. Perhaps what you cannot 'stomach' is the way you are being treated by your boss or colleagues at work, but once the stomach-ache goes away you return to work and carry on as before. In this case, the cause hasn't been removed, even though the symptom has been relieved. Soon the tension returns, and the stomach-ache comes back, or is replaced by some other, often more serious, symptom of stress. What is needed in this situation is a change of consciousness, a realisation that the situation at work must be tackled in a proactive way. This might mean being assertive – telling your work colleagues that you find their attitutude unacceptable, or talking to your boss about your dissatisfaction. It may even mean you need to look for another job that you would find more enjoyable and better suited to your skills and talents. Sometimes illness can be a 'wake-up' call to show us we're not on the right track.

Involve yourself in your own healing; take responsibility for your own health and well-being. Healing isn't confined to the physical body – it also affects the mind, the emotions and the spirit. Dr Usui taught the Reiki principles, as a means of encouraging people to be fully conscious of their own lives and how they were living them.

The Reiki Principles

The traditional history tells that Dr Usui received inspiration during meditation about the healing of the spirit through a conscious decision to take responsibility for one's own health and well-being, in order for the Reiki healing energies to have lasting results. He also gained insight into the way people will take for granted, or not value, those things which they receive too freely and easily. It is said that he was then given the five spiritual principles of Reiki to balance the physical healing. Interestingly, according to Frank Arjava Petter, the five principles of Reiki adopted by Dr Usui were originally suggested as guidelines for a fulfilled life by the Meiji Emperor of Japan during the period 1868 to 1912.

Just For Today

One of the most important aspects of the principles is the phrase *Just For Today*. Living in the moment, being aware of what is going on around you, forces you to live in the present, the only time over which you have any control, the moment of power. In fact most of us spend much of each day thinking about other times, such as:

☆ feeling angry, guilty, regretful or nostalgic about what we did yesterday, last week or last year; or

☆ feeling worried, hopeful, excited or apprehensive about what we're planning to do tonight, tomorrow, next week or next month.

Consider the thoughts that have been flitting through your mind even as you've been reading this book. Are they anything like these?

☆ 'What shall we have for tea tonight?'

☆ 'I wonder if I locked the car?'

☆ 'Did I put those papers I need in the bin by mistake?'

☆ 'I wonder if John/Jane is going to ring me?'

☆ Or perhaps you've been going through an inventory of

imperatives: 'I must ...'; 'I should ...'; 'I ought to ...'; 'Why didn't I ... ?'.

The past is gone, and the future hasn't arrived yet, so why not really pay attention to and enjoy whatever it is you are doing now? If you're not enjoying it, then ask yourself why you're doing it, and maybe do something else.

Living in the present can be so much more rewarding than constantly thinking about the past or the future. You can begin to *really* feel, see and hear what is going on around you. When did you last really look at the colour of a flower, touch a velvety petal, linger on the delicious scent? Can you even envisage doing that right now?

EXERCISE: LIVING IN THE MOMENT

Try this awareness-raising exercise for a few minutes, to use your senses to pick up all the sensations of the present moment.

☆ Find a comfortable place to sit, and spend a few moments settling down, perhaps by deepening and slowing your breathing, until you feel quite relaxed.

☆ Close your eyes and focus your attention on what you can hear around you. Really listen. What are the sounds? Birds singing, nearby traffic, a radio in the next room, a dog barking, a clock ticking, people's voices? Let your awareness spread out, and see if you can hear even more.

☆ Turn your attention to what you can smell. Breathe in the air slowly, letting the smells linger in your nostrils. What can you smell? The fragrance of fresh flowers, perfume, room freshener, or the smell of stale tobacco or sweaty clothes. Are there any food smells, perhaps baking bread or the aroma of fresh coffee? Open your mouth to let the air flow over your taste buds, and see if you can expand your sense of smell to distinguish even more odours around you.

☆ Next pay attention to your sense of touch. Are you aware of different parts of your body, or its weight in the chair? Can you feel the texture of your clothes against your skin, or the warmth of the sun or the softness of a breeze against your face? Feel your body moving as you breathe in and out. Perhaps tense the muscles in your shoulders and then let them relax, feeling the different sensations as they change.

☆ Now open your eyes and let yourself look around you. Notice light and shade, colours and shapes, patterns and designs. Pick out one colour, and notice the different shades and tones of that colour, from deep and dark to pale and light. If there is a plant nearby, examine the structure of its leaves, the way they join the main stem, the delicate formation of buds about to burst into new growth. Look down at your own hands, and see the texture and colour of the skin, the wrinkles around the knuckles, the smoothness of the nails, the myriad of lines in your palms, some deep, some light, some fine. Notice the shape of your palm, and the different lengths of your fingers. Have you ever paid this much attention to any part of your body before?

☆ Now spend a few moments integrating this experience. This is what your life is like at this moment in time. For a few minutes you have really paid attention to what is going on around you, to what you are doing. How does that feel? Have you ever felt so 'awake' to your surroundings before? This is truly living in the present!

☆ Just allow yourself a few moments to 'come round' from this heightened state of awareness, and then continue with whatever you had planned to do.

It would be difficult to maintain such a state of awareness all the time - you simply couldn't concentrate on anything else and your brain's interpretation of your senses would rapidly become overloaded. However, try this exercise fairly regularly to remind yourself of the sheer magic of living in a human body which gives us all these amazing sensations which we so readily take for granted.

In terms of living in the present, one saying sums it up:

> The past is history, the future is a mystery.
> Today is a gift, that's why it's called the present.

Let yourself enjoy today. It will never come again.

Just For Today, Do Not Anger

Anger is such a destructive emotion, and often we express our anger to those people we care about the most, so it hurts us as much as it hurts them. Anger is usually tied to expectations about what you believe should or should not be happening, or to responses about things which have happened in the past. But anger is a conscious choice, and is often just a habit. You've probably been reacting in a similar way in similar circumstances for years, but you can choose not to be angry.

Of course, you cannot avoid anger completely. That would be unrealistic. However, anger is only one of a whole gamut of responses at your disposal. Any of them might gain you a better result instead – but first you have to take a deep breath and let go of that habitual response. The old adage of counting to ten before speaking is pretty sensible!

Think of a situation in which you usually get angry. At such times we often blame the other person – 'You made me angry by ...' – but in reality you chose to be angry. Other people can't make you feel emotions. Their actions can cause you to react, but the type of reaction is up to you.

The most obvious way to change the tone of any situation is to talk about it calmly and rationally, expressing your feelings in a way that doesn't hurt the other person, communicating openly but not aggressively. It's about making a conscious choice to let go, and to embrace an attitude of forgiveness, understanding and conciliation, rather than anger, misunderstanding and confrontation. Of course it is important to acknowledge your anger. It is a valid emotion, and it is unhealthy to simply bottle it up without finding some release for it, but there are safer ways of expressing anger than shouting or screaming or saying things that afterwards you may deeply regret.

Physical activity is an excellent way of getting rid of anger – thumping a cushion, going for a brisk walk, swimming, or taking part in a vigorous sport such as squash. Other ways of releasing anger include singing (loudly!), painting, housework, or writing down your feelings in a poem or a letter and symbolically burning it, freeing your anger with the smoke. Sometimes talking things over with a friend to get things 'off your chest' is all it takes to gain a new perspective on a situation.

To let go of anger is to release what is blocking you from giving and receiving unconditional love. Perhaps it sounds like an oversimplification, but try it – *just for today*.

Just For Today, Do Not Worry

Worry is our usual response to a probable or possible event in the future, to something that might occur, but that often does not. Mark Twain once remarked that he had been through some terrible things in his life, some of which had actually happened! Our tendency is to put ourselves through hell in our minds, contemplating what could come to pass, yet if we look at the present moment, which is all we really have, there is no great problem at all.

Worrying can be a bad habit, so consider various situations where you might normally be anxious. A visit to the dentist might take as little as ten minutes, but some people put themselves through weeks of agony beforehand. If you're taking a test or attending an interview, worrying will not give you a better chance of success, but study and planning will. If you are having money problems, worrying isn't going to help either. If you can take some action, like visiting the bank manager, or asking a creditor for more time to pay, or seeking advice from the Citizens' Advice Bureau, then do it. If you can do nothing, then just 'let go, and let flow'.

I'm a firm believer that struggling and striving to control a situation just creates an energy cycle which makes things worse. When we let go and stop worrying about the situation, something good comes along to sort it out. That 'good' may be a person, useful advice or a helpful sum of money, and it's amazing how often just the right thing turns up. You can choose not to worry – *just for today*.

Honour Your Parents, Teachers and Elders

For years I thought I understood this principle. As I had been brought up to be polite I assumed I was already fulfilling its dictate, but I eventually came to understand that its influence is much wider. It really means we should honour and be grateful to everyone for the part they play in our lives: partners, friends, neighbours, colleagues, children, shop assistants, bus drivers – in fact, every person we meet, under any circumstances. Every interaction with another person is a potential learning experience. Shop assistants gossiping about last night's party instead of serving us are teaching us patience. A gang of teenage boys shouting obscenities in the street are teaching us tolerance. The tiny baby we hold in our arms is teaching us love.

We are continually making conscious choices when we make contact with people, choosing those from whom we wish to learn, those we want as friends, those we need to work with. And 'what goes around, comes around' – as you honour and respect other people, they will do the same for you, too.

Just for today, honour and respect everyone you meet, and also value yourself for the important difference you make to the universe.

Earn your living honestly

'Earning a living' refers to all types of work, from everyday tasks such as cooking a meal for yourself or your family, to working on self-development through meditation or reading inspirational books. We often confuse what we do with who we are, taking our sense of identity from the kind of job we have – or don't have. This is one of the major reasons why being labelled as 'unemployed' can be so stressful; if we only recognise ourselves for our job title, being jobless takes away our sense of self. We need to remember that we are human beings, not human doings! All of us are valuable and special. Every life, every person, has a role to play in the whole, and we all impact on each other in many different ways.

It is important to respect any 'job' we have chosen, and to honour ourselves by doing our best to create a feeling of satisfaction in that work. All work is valuable to the extent that we choose to value it, so value whatever work you do, in the home, at school or college, as voluntary work or as paid employment. Take satisfaction from even the simplest tasks. A well-known quotation says: 'Before enlightenment, chop wood, carry water; after enlightenment, chop wood, carry water.' No matter how spiritual your life may become, you still need to work in some manner to feed and clothe yourself, and to keep warm and live comfortably.

Being in the present means enjoying and valuing what you are doing right now and doing everything to the best of your ability. Doing your work honestly also means being honest with yourself, as well as with others, accepting yourself for who you are. *Just for today*, do your work honestly.

Show Gratitude to Every Living Thing

As part of the universal lifeforce you begin to feel more and more connected to 'All That Is'. As your consciousness is raised, you know instinctively that every living thing is a part of you, and that you are a part of it. Everything is a part of the Divine, God, the Source or whatever you choose to call it. We come to realise there is no place for prejudice, cruelty or indifference in a world where we are all connected and a part of the whole. All people, animals, birds, insects and plants have a vital role to play, and therefore they should be valued, respected and treated with kindness. We need to be grateful for our many blessings, but first we need to recognise what they are.

If life is difficult and we're going through a 'bad patch', we tend to see things from a very morose perspective and assume everything is bad. Even when life is relatively calm and happy we are often not aware of it, and take it very much for granted. Yet most of us in the West are living very good lives, even if they aren't perfect. Even if you have few material goods, there are still many things to be grateful for, from the beauty of a sunset to the warmth of an open fire, from the gentle touch of a lover to the sweet kiss of a small child.

I believe it is important to develop an 'attitude of gratitude', to constantly remind ourselves of the wonderful world we inhabit. Take time out of every day just to stand and stare, whether at the beauty of a flower or the happiness of a child at play. Develop an awareness of life, and what it means to live it. There may be ups and downs, and sometimes we'll be happy and sometimes we'll be sad, but every experience is valuable because it helps to make us who we are. So, *just for today*, show gratitude to every living thing, and give thanks for your many blessings.

6

Learning Reiki

Reiki is probably the simplest and easiest holistic healing method available. Anyone can learn to use Reiki, whatever their age or sex, religion or origin. 'Learning' Reiki is probably a misnomer, because the ability to let this healing energy flow through you is passed on from the Reiki Master to the student in a sacred ceremony of attunement or initiation. As soon as you have been attuned you have, and can use, Reiki. You don't need any specific knowledge or experience, just a willingness to let this healing energy flow through you, and a little time.

Attunements

The dictionary defines 'attune' as 'to bring into harmony'. The attunements are the way in which the Reiki Master helps to bring you into harmony with this healing energy by opening your chakras to create a channel to allow the Reiki to flow through you. Some Masters call this process an 'initiation' (which means 'allowing to begin'), as it is a sacred ceremony which creates a special link between you and the

Reiki source, initiating you into your new life with Reiki.

A Reiki attunement is an ancient spiritual empowerment, and as such, it is a powerful spiritual experience, although how it is experienced will vary from person to person, as the Rei, or God consciousness, guides the whole process, adjusting it to the needs of each individual. The sacred and spiritual process of channelling the Reiki through the Reiki Master into the student is usually carried out with the student seated in silent meditation with their eyes closed and their hands held in a prayer position. The attunement can be a very special experience, and afterwards, students often describe beautiful spiritual or mystical experiences or a feeling of complete peace.

The attunement is only the start of your connection to Reiki. Over the ensuing weeks and months, as you practise treating yourself and others, the flow of Reiki gains strength so that within six to eight weeks you are experiencing the full flow of energy. The more you use it, the better it flows, and once you have received a Reiki attunement you can use Reiki for the rest of your life. It doesn't wear off or wear out, as the supply of Reiki is inexhaustible. You can never lose the ability to channel it. If for some reason you don't use Reiki for a number of years you may think it isn't flowing because you have no sensation of it in your hands. Some people ask to be reattuned if this happens, but there is no need as it is still there, though you may need to practise to restore the full flow. If you choose to undertake a reattunement, it won't do any harm.

Reiki Training

If you want to channel Reiki for healing for the rest of your life, all you really need is First Degree, which allows you to access as much healing energy as you need at any time in any place. The quality of the Reiki does not alter with further attunements, so the Reiki from a person with First Degree Reiki is as good as the Reiki from a Master. If you proceed to higher degrees of attunement the vibrationary rate is heightened and you are able to tap into a higher, wider channel of Reiki, which enables even more Reiki to flow through you.

It is also important to understand that Reiki is not a knowledge-based system. Receiving Reiki is a spiritual empowerment, so the emphasis is not on acquiring more certificates or higher qualifications, but is about raising your consciousness and deepening your spiritual commitment to Reiki as a God-directed lifeforce energy. It is therefore only appropriate to take a Second Degree course if you are sure that you want to engage in further spiritual development through Reiki, in addition to learning some new and valuable techniques. Even more importantly, becoming a Reiki Master is not simply a means of gaining a higher qualification. It is a life-changing spiritual empowerment leading to many challenges as well as providing a powerful tool for personal and spiritual growth.

You do not have to go on to higher degrees once you have been to a Reiki First Degree class. With therapies such as aromatherapy or homoeopathy, you probably need to spend a long time acquiring knowledge and advanced qualifications in order to achieve what you want. With Reiki, you don't. You could spend a lifetime learning how to get the most out of First Degree; receiving the attunement is just the beginning. After that, every day of using Reiki can bring you new understanding. The vast majority of people in the worldwide Reiki community only have First Degree.

First Degree

This is the basic course suitable for everyone, whatever their age or background, from people who mainly wish to use Reiki on themselves, friends and family to those who wish to go on to become practitioners. It is usually held over a weekend or sometimes over four afternoons or evenings (normally a minimum of 12 hours of teaching). Many Masters offer a free introductory talk some time before the course, so that you can find out more about it, have a chance to experience Reiki for yourself, and be sure that the course is right for you.

Reiki First Degree courses traditionally include four attunements and cover a comprehensive explanation of the Usui System of Reiki Natural Healing, including the story of how it was rediscovered by Dr Usui. Full training should be given in the basic form of treatment: hand positions on the head and body for treating yourself and others, and advice on how to give treatments for injuries or accidents. Plenty of time is usually allowed for practising on yourself and other students under the supervision of the Reiki Master. Expect to be encouraged to ask questions and share your experiences during the course.

There are variations in teaching methods. Some Masters conduct only one integrated attunement on each student. This works perfectly well, although there are clearly differences. In the traditional method the energy is allowed to build up slowly and gently over several sessions, whereas the integrated method 'delivers' the energy all at once. It also means, of course, that you have the opportunity for only one lovely spiritual experience, rather than four. The hand positions for treatment may also vary from one Master to another, depending upon how they were taught, and many

Masters teach additional hand positions for specific purposes.

Meditations, chanting, group treatments, aura and chakra work may also be included, or a Master may choose to place particular emphasis on treating animals or working on healing the environment. Though none of these aspects are strictly necessary, they can make the course an even more interesting experience for some students.

Second Degree

This course is traditionally only available to those people who have already completed First Degree and have a minimum of three months' practice. It is recommended for people who want to become Reiki practitioners, and for those who wish to use Reiki more effectively on their own inner development. The course normally takes two days (or four sessions) and includes a further energy attunement to intensify your inner healing channel – to as much as four times that received with First Degree. Many people find it a very profound experience. You are taught three sacred symbols and their mantras (see page 74), and a range of special techniques which use one or more of these symbols, including:

☆ intensifying the energy flow in 'hands-on' treatments;

☆ distant (or absent) healing;

☆ healing life situations;

☆ dealing with deep-seated emotional and mental problems;

☆ using Reiki for your own further personal development;

☆ healing the planet.

Practice time should be available on the course, but participants should also expect to allocate time over the following months to practise both hands-on and distant treatments. Many Masters will not issue a Second Degree certificate until this extra practice has been conducted.

Some Masters cover additional topics and techniques such as: cleansing the aura with smudge, which is a blend of special herbs (usually desert sage, lavender and cedar); developing sensitivity in your hands to enable you to scan the aura for energy variations; meditations to meet your Reiki spirit guides; empowering affirmations and goals with Reiki; and cleansing crystals or spaces using Reiki. Some of these are not strictly necessary, but often they enhance the experience for students and show them just part of the immense potential of Reiki at this level.

Occasionally some Reiki Masters hold extra one- or two-day courses for students who have already had some experience of using the Second Degree symbols, to enable them to teach these and other special techniques.

Third Degree

This is the level of a Reiki Master, intended for those who have already practised at Second Degree level for several years, usually as practitioners, and who feel drawn to demonstrate their commitment to Reiki by learning more advanced techniques and becoming a Master. The traditional training is extensive, usually taking at least a year working individually with a Master, learning and practising all aspects of Reiki. This level includes a further symbol and mantra, and a further attunement enhancing the ability to channel Reiki to up to ten times that at Reiki Second Degree. The Third Degree student should also have the opportunity to learn how to organise Reiki classes and to practise teaching

First and Second Degree classes under the supervision of the Master. There is also usually some personal work between Master and student on inner awareness and spiritual growth, so that the student fully understands the commitment required by the role of Reiki Master. It is expected that a Master will teach only the first two levels of Reiki for at least two or three years in order to gain the considerable experience necessary to teach the Master level.

It is important to understand the distinction between the Master level and the other two levels. Becoming a Reiki Master is not simply gaining a higher qualification, but a commitment to the mastery of Reiki, and a lifelong task. At Master level, working on your spiritual development is no longer optional – it is essential – and this inevitably engenders considerable changes, perhaps to your diet, lifestyle, job, relationships, home, or inner life. If you are content with the life you have now, don't bother becoming a Reiki Master! A Reiki Master must possess integrity, dedication and motivation. Examine your rationale for becoming a Master, and be sure that it is what you really want to do, because you will be doing it for the rest of your life!

Reiki is a spiritual discipline, but unlike most other spiritual disciplines it does not take years of study and dedication before you are granted access to it. Anyone can take Reiki, regardless of their age, gender, nationality, spiritual background or beliefs.

The traditional method of training Reiki Masters over one or two years was designed to prepare people for the responsibilities of the role, and to assess their readiness. The high fees that have traditionally been charged were also designed to encourage real commitment. As it was difficult to become a Reiki Master, only those who were really keen to follow this particular spiritual path were attracted to it.

Now an increasing number of independent Reiki Masters teach this level as a course, rather than by the apprenticeship method, and their charges are considerably lower. They also sometimes split the courses into two levels – Reiki Master (or Master Practitioner) and Reiki Master/Teacher. The courses usually include an additional attunement and several extra symbols and mantras from a different healing tradition, plus other techniques.

A short course isn't necessarily the easy route. Becoming a Reiki Master is just the beginning of a tremendously interesting, exciting and challenging journey towards mastery of this amazingly powerful, mysterious healing energy. Ten, or twenty, or thirty years from now you will still be on that journey ... still learning, still growing, still changing, with the help of Reiki. Once you have received the Master attunement you have taken a vital step on your spiritual path, and there is no way to turn round and undo it.

The Reiki Symbols

There are four Reiki symbols used in the Usui System of Natural Healing. These are calligraphic symbols, each of which has a secret name (a sacred mantra) and another public name by which it is commonly known. Three symbols are taught to Reiki Second Degree students, and the fourth symbol is taught only to Reiki Masters.

The Power Symbol: This increases the power of Reiki and can be used for a variety of purposes including clearing spaces of negative energies, and protecting yourself or anything else you value.

The Mental Symbol: This is used mainly for healing

mental and emotional problems and their causes. It balances the left and right sides of the brain, and can improve the memory and enhance learning capacity.

The Distant Symbol: This is used for absent healing. It cuts through time and space, enabling Reiki (including a full Reiki treatment) to be sent to anyone, anywhere, at any time. This symbol bridges time, so Reiki can also be sent into the past or the future.

The Master Symbol: This is only taught to Reiki Masters, and is used during the attunement process to connect the student with the Reiki source.

The symbols and their mantras are not printed here because they are sacred and are meant to be kept secret. The 'secretness' of the Reiki symbols has been misunderstood in the West where the word 'secret' is seen as shameful. In contrast, in the East the words sacred and secret are interconnected both culturally and experientially. Perhaps a better way of expressing this aspect of Reiki is to see the symbols as something deeply spiritual and intrinsically personal, and therefore something which is kept private.

Time and Money

The traditional way to progress through Reiki was to spend time allowing the energy to work with you to raise your vibrationary frequencies until you were ready to take the next level. This usually meant waiting at least three months after a First Degree course before going on to Second Degree. Many people used to wait much longer than that. It was then normal to work with Reiki as a practitioner for several years before starting Master training. At the end of the training a Master would have at least five years' experience of Reiki to offer their potential students. They would also be encouraged to wait perhaps another year, working with the Master level energy, before starting to run their own classes.

Now it is relatively easy to find a Master who will allow you to progress very rapidly through the levels of Reiki, doing First and Second Degree in the same weekend, and perhaps only weeks or months later taking the Master level. This accelerated training has its own challenges, because your physical body doesn't have time to adjust to the increased energetic frequencies brought by each level of attunement. This means that the clearing-out process over the following weeks and months (or years, in the case of the Master level) is intense and often uncomfortable. This is a very powerful energy, and while it always works for your highest good, it doesn't always work the way you would like it to! Life changes often happen at a remarkably rapid pace, and healing crises can occur as the energy forces you to adjust quickly to the spiritual path you have chosen. It is your choice whether to take Reiki slowly over several years, or quickly over several months. Either way, Reiki will flow through you to raise your consciousness and activate your personal and spiritual development. Some people are happiest when they have time to learn from and absorb changes slowly, while others love the adrenalin rush of the 'fast track' and are happy to deal with the consequences.

Independent Reiki Masters tend to charge lower prices than those who belong to the Reiki Alliance. However don't let cost be the only criteria by which you make your choice when deciding which course to go on, or which Master to train with. Even if you have little money to spare, and think you couldn't possibly afford to pay some of the larger sums required, I can assure you that if it is right for you to learn from a particular Master the relevant amount of money will come to you somehow. Abundance Theory proposes that the universe is totally abundant, and will always give us what we need. (Note that I said 'need', not 'want'). Many of my students, and those of other Masters I know, have told amazing stories about how the exact amount of money came to them, usually at the last minute, from sources such as unexpected legacies or forgotten insurance policies – and even a lottery win. You have to trust and be open to the ways in which the money can come to you.

Choosing a Reiki Master

Every Reiki Master is unique. Each one brings something of themselves to the way they teach. Just as I believe Reiki finds you at precisely the right time in your life, rather than you finding it, I believe you always find the right Reiki Master too. Follow your intuition and recommendations from people you know, and use a smattering of common sense! Someone with years of experience of teaching Reiki is probably (although not always) going to be better at it than someone who has just completed their training. A Reiki Master who previously spent years working as a Reiki practitioner can offer better advice on how to treat clients than one who has only treated family and friends. Being in a class of 10 or 12 people will allow you to gain more personal attention than a class for 30, 50 or 80.

Allow yourself to be drawn to the right person, who will usually be someone you like, respect and feel has integrity, behaves in a caring and supportive manner and has the kind of attitudes and beliefs with which you feel comfortable. Be aware of the issues most important to you. Do you want someone with a very spiritual approach, or would you prefer someone particularly practical and down-to-earth? Are you looking for one-to-one training, or would you prefer to be part of a class? Do you like to take your time and practise each level before moving on, or are you looking for 'fast-track' training – and if so, why? Is price the most important factor, or do you trust the universe to provide the money you need for whichever Master you like best?

Don't be afraid to ask questions, such as:

☆ How long have they been doing Reiki? i.e., when did they do First Degree?

☆ How long have they been a Reiki Master, and what is their lineage?

☆ How long do the classes last, and what is covered in each class?

☆ How many students are in a typical class?

☆ How long do they advise you to wait between each level of training?

☆ Will the training be in Usui Reiki? Do they also teach other forms of Reiki?

☆ How much do they charge for the training? Why do they charge that amount?

☆ What support do they offer to students after the course ends?

☆ Do they have a Reiki sharing group in your area that you could join?

☆ Will you get a certificate?

☆ Do they hold an introductory evening where you can find out more about Reiki?

Also ask yourself why you want to do Reiki. Is it for interest? For self-healing? So that you can help others? As a new career? To help you to grow personally and spiritually? Your answers should help you to find a Master. But in the end all you can do is follow your heart, and trust that the experience will be the right one for you. Allow the energy to lead you, trust yourself to make the right decision, and then go for it!

Preparing for a Reiki Course

When you choose to take Reiki, at whatever level, it means you have reached a significant stage on your life path. A Reiki attunement is a very special experience that can be enhanced if you bring your physical, mental, emotional and spiritual bodies into harmony and balance during the week before a course commences. Some aspects of our normal eating habits and busy life-styles are not particularly conducive to this balance, so the following suggestions are optional. Please follow them if you feel guided to do so.

☆ Many people find it very helpful to go on a gentle 'detox' diet for a few days before an attunement. This basically means eating only raw fresh vegetables and fruit (preferably organic) and drinking only water.

☆ If you are accustomed to fasting, you might wish to start with 24 hours on a water or fruit/vegetable juice fast.

☆ If that all sounds a bit too drastic, then even if you are not a vegetarian you may find it helpful to cut out meat and fish for a few days before the course, substituting lots of fresh organic fruit and vegetables instead, as this helps to cleanse your physical system. (Meat and fish may contain small quantities of drugs or other toxins.) Cutting down on or eliminating processed foods is helpful, too, as most contain preservatives or additives.

☆ It is extremely beneficial to drink more water than usual. Six to eight glasses a day (about two litres) is recommended, in addition to any other drinks. Check with your doctor if you have any reason to suspect that a change of diet or increased water intake could be detrimental.

☆ It is best to eliminate alcohol for a few days before and after the attunements, and during the Reiki course itself. Try to minimise your consumption of caffeine drinks, sweets and chocolate.

☆ If you smoke, try to cut down for several days beforehand. Smoke as little as possible during and immediately after the course.

☆ Try to reduce or eliminate altogether the time you spend in any activities or situations which carry negative energy (this includes watching TV news, or violent or fear-inducing programmes or films; listening to loud music, reading newspapers).

☆ Actively release any negative emotions such as anger, fear, jealousy or hatred by imagining them in a bubble of light which you allow to float up to the universe to be healed. Then imagine yourself in a bubble of light as a sacred space. (You can use the visualisation at the end of this chapter.)

☆ Try to spend some time quietly in meditation, or taking quiet walks in the park or countryside, as these are useful activities to 'destress' you so that you will be more in tune with the nature of the course.

For the course itself, you will probably find it best to wear comfortable, loose clothing – tracksuits, leggings, T-shirts, sweatshirts or similar are ideal, as they don't have tight waistbands. Wearing layers is helpful, too, as some people find they get very hot when the Reiki energy is flowing through them! Some Masters provide a manual or course notes, but you will almost certainly find it useful to take along a notebook and pen.

Whichever Reiki course you attend, you will find that you will be sharing an interesting, empowering and enjoyable time with like-minded people.

After the Reiki Course

Some people experience a shift in consciousness immediately after a Reiki course, experiencing colours and sounds more intensely, feeling a buzzing or heightened sensitivity in the Crown chakra or a sense of floating or even slight lightheadedness. If this does happen, do accept it as absolutely normal. Any such sensations usually fade after a short time. Many people find they are very hungry during and after a Reiki course, or that they need more sleep than usual. Others, conversely, have extra energy. Most people feel on a 'high' when they've finished the course, though, so I would recommend that you slip back into normal life as gently as possible afterwards. This may not be easy, as often the courses are held at the weekend and you may have to return to work on the Monday. If you do have the chance to take an extra day off, just allow yourself to 'come down' slowly, perhaps sleeping longer and then spending the day doing gentle things like walking, reading, meditating or listening to relaxing music.

In order to raise the vibrationary rate at which you operate at each level of attunement, there has to be a clearing of old physical, mental, emotional and spiritual patterns and thoughts that inhibit the growth of consciousness. One of the major effects, therefore, is what is called the 21-day clearing cycle, where your whole energy body is cleansed and cleared by the Reiki.

21-Day Clearing Cycle

During the first week after a Reiki course, this clearing takes place gradually by proceeding up through the chakras – the Root or Base chakra on day one, the Sacral chakra on day two, and so on up to the Crown chakra on day seven. During the second and third weeks this clearing is repeated in the same way – Base chakra on day one, Sacral chakra on day two, and so on. I usually describe this as a sort of energetic 'spring cleaning' where the Reiki gently flows through and breaks down the blockages in your whole energy system.

As the blocks preventing your progress are brought forward, they need to be released by your physical, emotional, mental and spiritual bodies. The effects of this release can vary from making you feel more emotional or irritable than usual, to giving you the urge to laugh or cry, to producing a sense of detachment and the need to spend more time alone. Sometimes you may experience a temporary 'healing crisis', such as a cold, but this is a perfectly natural way to release toxins out of the body (if a little uncomfortable). However, this does not always happen, so don't turn it into a self-fulfilling prophecy! Realise that Reiki always works for the highest good, so trust Reiki to know what's best and to do it. You can make the whole process much easier for yourself, by following these suggestions:

☆ It is really important to do a full self-treatment (at least half an hour) every day during this clearing cycle.

☆ It is equally important to drink much more water than usual – at least four more glasses a day than usual, preferably six or eight (approximately two litres). This needs to be pure water (other drinks like tea, coffee, cordials, or fizzy drinks don't count) but it can be either bottled or tap water. (Sparkling water is fine, so long as it isn't flavoured.) (If you have any health problems related to water retention, please seek medical advice before drinking extra water.)

☆ You may also find it useful to repeat the Reiki principles to yourself daily.

Over the three weeks you will probably notice a gradual strengthening of the Reiki as you use it. You may notice other changes in yourself too. For this purpose it is useful to keep a journal of your 'Reiki journey' for the first few weeks, to record what you experience during self-treatment, or during treatments of friends, family, pets or plants. You may also find it a good idea to describe any vivid dreams, emotional episodes, feelings, meditations or changes you feel are taking place in yourself. You may be able to link them to the particular chakra being cleared on that day.

This journal is a self-exploratory document to help you experience Reiki in a very personal and positive way. You don't have to share it with anyone, although of course you could discuss it with your Reiki Master afterwards if you wish.

EXERCISE: VISUALISATION TO PREPARE FOR A REIKI ATTUNEMENT

One of the recommended ways to prepare for a Reiki attunement is letting go of negative emotions, and this visualisation will help you to do this. Preparing for a Reiki course isn't the only time to let go of negative emotions, so this visualisation can be used at other times too.

You can also substitute different emotions for the ones mentioned in the visualisation if you particularly want to work on other issues such as resentment or jealousy. Before you begin, you will need to be in a comfortable, quiet place where you won't be disturbed, and it would be helpful to follow through the relaxation stage of the visualisation to cleanse your aura on page 29 before starting this particular guided imagery.

☆ Relax all parts of the body.

☆ Begin to imagine that you are standing on a path in sunlit woodland at the foot of a beautiful mountain. Use all your senses to connect with this image. Look down at your feet to see what kind of shoes you are wearing. Look up at the blue sky, feel the warmth of the sun on your face, sense a gentle breeze ruffling your hair. Put out your hand to touch something – the rough bark of a tree, or the softness of a blade of grass. Smell the pine-scented air.

☆ Start to walk along the path, seeing or sensing the beautiful trees around you as the path begins to wind upwards. As you are walking, you feel that the path is becoming narrower, and the woodland is becoming thicker and darker, and you suddenly realise that you are carrying a very heavy bag.

☆ Stop for a moment, and take off the bag to examine the contents. You see that this bag is labelled 'Fear', and when you look inside you can see or sense images of all those things which make you fearful. You realise that you don't have to carry this heavy burden of fear around with you any longer. You can choose to leave it here beside the woodland path, and move on, knowing that if you really need any of these fears you can choose to pick up any of them from this bag on your way back down the mountain.

☆ Now you stride on up the path. The trees become thinner and the sun warms you as you climb further, but the path is becoming steeper, and you realise that you are carrying other heavy bags on your back. You go a little further and decide that it's time to examine one of the other bags that you have brought along, so you take off the one labelled 'Anger'. Looking inside, you see or sense images of people or situations that frequently trigger angry emotions in you, but as you look at them you realise that you can choose not to react to these triggers any more. You can leave all your anger in this bag, so you place it down and leave it beside the path. Such emotions are no longer appropriate for you on this journey, but you know that you can pick them up later if you wish.

☆ You continue climbing, and now you are above the trees. The sun is getting hotter and hotter, and you eagerly take off another bag to look inside it. This bag is labelled 'Guilt', and inside it you find images of all the times when you have felt guilty or jealous or resentful or grudging or possessive. Now you realise that you can let go of those feelings, so you put down the bag and leave it beside the path, feeling much lighter as you step out on the path again, although you know that if you wish to you may pick up any of these feelings again on your way back down the mountain.

☆ Higher and higher you climb. Now you are almost at the top of the mountain, but the way is really steep, and you have another bag that is becoming very, very heavy. You decide to take it off, and see that it is labelled 'Worry'. Inside you can see or sense all those things you worry about, all the thoughts which have kept you awake at night, the judgements and prejudices and attitudes which have held you back – tangled together in a great heap. With a feeling of great relief, you realise that you can also leave all your worries bundled up in this bag, and you place it beside the path, knowing that if any of these worries are necessary, you can pick them up again on your way back.

☆ Now you just have a little way to go, but the path has

become dangerously narrow and so steep that you are having to scramble up the rocks. The last bag on your back has become too cumbersome and heavy to continue with, so you take it off and gratefully put it on the ground. You notice that it is labelled 'Hatred', and when you look inside you are surprised to find any images of such a strong emotion, yet in the darkest recesses of your mind there are people and incidents that have triggered this feeling in you, but now you can release this negative emotion by leaving this bag, like the others, beside the path.

☆ You now feel so light that the path is easy. You find yourself right at the top of the mountain, and as you stand there the streams of sunlight become beautiful beams of rainbow-coloured light, and you feel your whole body and energy field suffused with glorious colour as each chakra and each layer of your aura is cleansed of negativity, leaving you feeling peaceful yet refreshed and grateful to be so vibrantly alive.

☆ The rainbow light recedes, and you begin to make your way back down the mountain. As you come to the last bag you left beside the path you realise that you don't need to pick up any negative emotions any more, and you find that the bag has changed, and instead of 'Hatred' the label now says 'Love', so you pick it up and find that it is as light as a feather. Moving further down the path you come to the next bag, and find that the label 'Worry' has been replaced with 'Joy', and you pick it up and find that it, too, is as light as a feather. Walking quickly now, you reach the next bag and find that the label has changed from 'Guilt' to 'Freedom' and you swing it easily on to your shoulder and move even more quickly down the path. As you reach the next bag you see that the 'Anger' label has changed to 'Peace' so you eagerly pick it up and begin to run down the path. When you reach the very first bag you put down, which had been labelled 'Fear', you find it has been replaced by 'Trust', and you happily pick it up and carry it lightly with the rest.

☆ As you reach the bottom of the mountain, where you first began, you look around you with a new appreciation of the beauty surrounding you – the bright colours, the warm sunlight, the delicious scents in the breeze – and you sit down on the grass and spread out around you the bags you have brought back down the mountain ... Love, Joy, Freedom, Peace and Trust. Each is full, yet they weigh hardly anything at all. You realise that you can choose to release any negative emotions, and fill your life with these and other positive emotions and feelings from now on, allowing you to move lightly through life.

☆ And now your awareness slowly begins to return, and you can hear the sounds around you, and become aware of your body again, and you may want to stretch a little, or wriggle your fingers and toes. Then, whenever you are ready, you can open your eyes and feel relaxed, yet fully awake and alert.

7

Self-Healing
With Reiki

Self-healing is one of the most important aspects of Reiki, and is
certainly the major focus of Reiki at First Degree level. It is an act
of self-love to give yourself a Reiki treatment every day, to give
yourself that priority to spend time with yourself. Because Reiki
works holistically, it will also support any other aspects of a self-
healing programme. However, a self-treatment is only part of
the story. As Reiki works holistically, your use of it helps healing
to take place in each of the four bodies – physical, emotional,
mental and spiritual – for the rest of your life.

Essentially, all healing is self-healing. Reiki is no cure-all.
It involves you in your own healing, encouraging you to take
responsibility for your own wholeness and health. Bringing
Reiki into yourself regularly begins the process of dislodging
blocks and obstacles within your energy system. As they are
removed they come to the surface for review, which often
means that memories of past events suddenly come into your
mind, or that you start to have very vivid dreams. You don't
need to become overly identified with them – simply
acknowledge them and let them go. (Imagining them in a

pink bubble, and seeing that bubble rise up into the sky and beyond to the universe for healing, is a good means of release.) Occasionally you may even find that previous events or situations recur, so you might feel that old problems have come back to plague you! You need to understand that this can be a necessary part of the process, and that you can use Reiki to heal, harmonise and balance these old feelings and fears simply by intending that this should happen. Presently you will feel better than you have ever felt before, as you rid yourself of years of blocked or stagnant energy.

Reiki Hand Positions For Self-Treatment

A Reiki self-treatment can be carried out either sitting or lying down, and the hand positions basically follow the chakras down the body, first down the front and then down the back, so it is quite easy to remember them. Once you have practised them for a while they will become second nature. Each hand position should feel comfortable, so if you have any shoulder, arm or hand mobility problems, please adapt the position to suit yourself and intend that the Reiki should go to the appropriate place. Your hands should be held still in each position for between two and five minutes, depending upon how much time you are able to allocate to a self-treatment. (I find it easiest to count the seconds silently – it turns the treatment into a type of meditation and I prefer to keep my eyes closed, so I can't see a clock.) If any area appears to need longer (i.e. your hands are still reacting with heat or tingling) then it is OK to continue for as long as seems appropriate.

If you have very little time, just one minute in each hand position is better than not doing it at all! A little Reiki is better than none, and a lot of Reiki is better than a little! You should consider why you cannot give yourself enough time to do a self-treatment. If you gave each hand position about two and a half minutes the whole treatment would only take half an hour. Why are you unable to spare half an hour for yourself? Are you living life at too hectic a pace? Are you giving your needs too little priority, rushing around after everyone else instead?

Front of Body

1 One hand held loosely over each eye.
2 One hand held loosely over each ear.
3 Both hands next to each other at the back of the head.
4 One hand on top of the other, covering the throat *or*
4A One hand on each side of the neck.
5 Both hands crossed in the centre of the chest *or*
5A One hand slightly above each breast.
6 One hand on each side of solar plexus (midriff).
7 One hand on each side of the navel/waist area.
8 Hands in a V-shape sloping down diagonally on pelvic area.

Back of body

9 One hand on top of each shoulder.
10 Both hands above the waist, as high up the back as is comfortable.
11 Both hands at waist level.
12 One hand on each buttock.
(13) One hand on top, and one hand below the left or right foot.
(14) One hand on top, one below the other foot.

It is optional to give Reiki to the thighs, knees, calves, ankles and feet, or to the upper arms, elbows, forearms, wrists, hands or fingers. If you have a health problem in one of these

1

2

3

4

4A

5

5A

6

(continued)

Traditional Reiki hand positions for self-treatment.

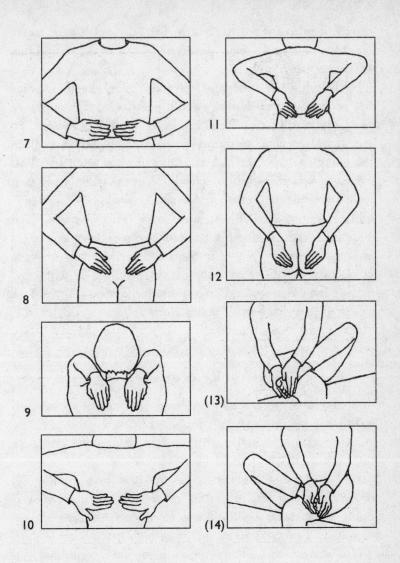

places, it makes sense to treat it. I usually finish with treatment for each foot – hand positions 13 and 14 – as I find this very energising.

Although a self-treatment every day is an excellent practice to promote self-healing, don't feel that it is the only way to give yourself Reiki. Reiki can be as flexible as you are, so you can place your hands anywhere on your body and allow the energy to flow through you anywhere, at any time. You can Reiki yourself while watching TV, at the cinema, waiting for a bus or sitting in the car during a traffic jam – the possibilities are endless. If you have some time to spare, give yourself Reiki. It doesn't require any conscious effort on your part. Simply put your hands on a convenient part of your body – your chest, solar plexus, stomach or thighs are usually the easiest – and intend that Reiki should flow. You can then feel that you're doing yourself some good, even if you're being a couch potato!

Taking Responsibility

The idea that we are all responsible for creating our own health has become part of popular culture in the past ten years or so, but it invites confusion. Many people interpret this to mean that we ourselves are to blame if we develop disease, but we should never *blame* ourselves for becoming ill, or for not being able to heal or instantly cure ourselves. We don't consciously invite illness in. Factors causing illness operate at a subconscious, energy or higher-self level.

The word responsibility means 'being able to respond', in this case meaning responding to your body's messages, learning from them and moving forward with a better understanding of what your body needs and what you, as a whole, need in your life. It also means treating your body and your whole self with love and respect, which usually means that you have to be willing to make changes in your life. Change is hardest when it is being resisted. When we actively seek change it is an exciting adventure; when we resist it, it becomes fearful.

You can help yourself to change by taking a good, hard look at your life-style to see if it is hindering or helping you to achieve optimum holistic health. Are you eating a healthy diet, or gorging on monosodium glutamate day after day? Are your major relationships healthy and loving, or stressful and tense? Are you happy with your job, or do you really yearn to do something else? Do you have time to indulge in hobbies and interests that add to your life? Do you think life is fun, or do you find it a struggle? Basically, the only person who can change your life is yourself. (Several books recommended in the Further Reading section illustrate different ways to change your life for the better.)

It can also be helpful to clear out your life on a practical level. Do a really thorough spring clean, regardless of the season. Go through cupboards, drawers, shelves, wardrobes, old suitcases, attics and basements – and don't forget your workplace, either. In your home, throw out or give away or sell everything that you don't love or no longer use.

Reiki can achieve the most amazing things, but it needs a willingness on the part of the person receiving it to allow changes in life-style, attitude, and ways of being, so that the healing can be completed and fully integrated into that person's life.

Developing a Self-Healing Programme

In addition to giving yourself Reiki every day, you might wish to put yourself on a wider programme to encourage overall health. The Reiki you give yourself will help substantially to support you in this. Any self-healing needs to be holistic, so you will need to deal with all aspects of yourself – physical, mental, emotional and spiritual. It is also useful to consider environmental aspects. The following suggestions outline key aspects to be considered and practical steps to be taken.

The Physical Body

Learn to be grateful for your physical body, the vehicle you have chosen to live in for this life. Like any vehicle, it needs good maintenance, tender loving care and a few words of appreciation every now and then to keep it running sweetly! The sensible way to help your physical body to achieve optimum health is to get enough sleep, eat a healthy, nutritious diet, drink plenty of water, take sufficient exercise and restrict your intake of harmful substances. It is also important to listen to your body's messages and to actively follow up on what you have learned, making the necessary changes to the way you live.

What is your body image? Do you like your body? You need to work on clearing out any negative self-beliefs, such as thinking you are too fat, too thin, too tall or too short. Start accepting and loving your body, appreciating it for the fine job it does, praising it instead of complaining about it, and giving it the priority in your life that it deserves.

A number of therapies have stimulating yet relaxing effects on the body, and could become part of your self-healing programme alongside Reiki: massage, aromatherapy, reflexology, shiatsu.

The Emotional Body

Your emotional body reacts to every emotion you experience,

so it makes sense to work on releasing negative feelings such as anger, jealousy, resentment or guilt and replace them with positive ones such as love, compassion, freedom and happiness. Try to spend as little time as possible in negative situations or with negative people. Work at improving all your relationships, from family and partner to friends and colleagues. It is important to acknowledge your feelings. Learn to express them sensitively but effectively, harnessing the creative, positive energy of your emotions. Do things you enjoy, build some creativity into your life, give yourself treats, and simply have fun.

Other practical steps can improve your emotional health. Sometimes we need outside help, so counselling, psychotherapy or hypnotherapy might be a good step forward. Other methods you could explore are neuro-linguistic programming (NLP), transactional analysis (TA) or family therapy. You can also use visualisations and affirmations to help with emotional problems.

The Mental Body

Your thought energy is what creates your life, attracting to you those things you think about, so it is vital to use your mind constructively and positively, acknowledging and then letting go of negative thoughts. The key is to live in the present, rather than in the past or future. Spend time reviewing your thought patterns, beliefs, attitudes and concepts, and dispose of those no longer useful to you, such as prejudice, intolerance, bigotry, or judgemental criteria. Do your best to cut down on the stress in your life (whether it is home- or work-based stress) by developing a more laid-back approach. Most of us get bogged down in trivia for 80 per cent of our time, spending only 20 per cent on what is really important. Prioritise everything you have to do and practise good time management and you'll release lots of time to do things you want to do, so you can develop the habit of giving time to yourself.

Practical steps to relaxation – the key to a stable and rested mental body – are plenty of sleep and regular meditation (15 minutes a day is fine). Also, treat yourself to a massage, aromatherapy or reflexology treatment as regularly as your budget will allow, and perhaps learn tai chi or yoga for gentle, meditative exercise. Some other methods for self-healing of the mental body are: Bach flower remedies, visualisations, affirmations, NLP and psychotherapy.

The Spiritual Body

The development of spiritual awareness gives your life meaning, so you need to examine your attitudes to spirituality and particular religions. What are your personal ideas about life and death? What are your feelings about other people's beliefs? Do you feel happy to develop your own personal spiritual beliefs? Or would you feel more comfortable exploring different religions until you found something which felt right?

The essential need of the spiritual body is to develop an unconditional loving relationship with yourself as part of the Divine. Practical steps include: reading inspirational books, meditation, visualisation, sound healing (e.g. chanting or toning), exploring your creativity and spending time in nature.

Environmental Factors

The environment can have a serious impact on your health. Various theories and environmental and ecological issues are significant:

Geopathic Stress The word 'geopathic' comes from the Greek 'geo', meaning 'of the Earth', and 'pathos', which describes suffering or disease. Over the last 20 years in particular, people have become more aware – and more wary – about the effects of energies emanating from natural or human-made sources. A considerable body of research material now confirms that people, animals and plants are affected physiologically (and probably in other ways) by these energies. The World Health Organisation cites that humans are now being bombarded with 200,000 times more electro-magnectic pollution than our prehistoric ancestors!

There are a variety of sources for geopathic energy, such as the Earth's magnetic field, which includes Earth energies such as ley lines and Curry lines (so called because they were discovered by Dr Manfred Curry). In addition, natural disturbances like geological faults, ore masses and under-ground water can affect us too. Human-made disturbances such as mining, underground utilities, and electromagnetic energy sources – like overhead power lines, radio and TV waves, microwaves, computer VDUs and other electrical equipment – are known to have a detrimental effect. Avoid places with overhead electricity cables or power-generating equipment, and switch off at the socket all electrical appli-ances unless you are using them.

Feng Shui Feng Shui is the ancient Eastern art of place-ment for balancing and harmonising the flow of natural energies in our homes or workplaces to create beneficial effects on our lives. The best advice is to keep your house or workplace clean and tidy all the time. Clear the clutter by throwing out things you don't need any more, which means everything you don't use, or don't love! This will immedi-ately improve the energies in your home or workspace, and have a positive impact on the way you feel, too. Other simple improvements can be effected by growing healthy plants all around your home, and keeping colours harmonious.

Activities to Encourage Self-Healing

One of the best activities to encourage self-healing is meditation. In all forms meditation has a focus and a quietening of the mind that at first simply reduces and then eventually eliminates the chatter of daily life and the stresses of our environment, so providing a haven within which we are free to connect with our inner being. It helps us to overcome problems and illusions that we create for ourselves and which we allow others to create for us, and to deal with habits that hold us back. Meditation allows us to go beyond the everyday, into who we really are. Focusing and an awareness of being in the moment changes brain activity, leading to a paradoxical opening of ourselves to the joy of the Universe.

There are many methods of meditation, of which visualisation, or guided meditation, is just one. Other types include:

☆ Chanting, toning or singing using repeated simple phrases or mantras;

☆ Transcendental meditation (going beyond the individual);

☆ Seeking the 'great void' or Nirvana (as in Buddhism);

☆ Meditation on objects, such as feathers or stones;

☆ Meditation on symbols, such as icons or mandalas;

☆ Meditation on candle flames;

☆ Meditation on the four elements: earth, air, fire and water (this is found in both Eastern and Western spiritual traditions).

All methods of meditation are equally valid. Try out several as you search for the method which suits you the best.

The following visualisation is designed to allow you to become much more aware of your physical body, deepening the two-way communication between body and mind. The physical body can 'store' emotions, blocks and pain that can lead to physical ailments if they are not cleared in some way. This visualisation gives you the opportunity to examine your whole body, allowing you to become aware of which parts need special attention, so that you can bring Reiki and/or healing light to where it is needed.

In addition, the visualisation gives you the time to value your wonderful, physical body and to recognise its importance in your life and spiritual journey. Start with the breathing exercise on page 30. This visualisation is probably best carried out while lying down, as it can induce a very deep state of relaxation.

EXERCISE: KNOW YOUR BODY

☆ Imagine a column of white light coming from the Universe or the Divine, down into the Crown chakra at the top of your head. Watch the light surround your whole body. Imagine you are breathing in the light, and you follow this light into your lungs and then up to the top of your head, and at the top of your head you allow it to flow around the skull and you notice all the bones and sockets of the skull. Then allow it to flow down into the vertebrae, the bones of the neck and back-bone, into the collar bone and the shoulder, then down the arms and through the wrist and into the fingers. Then take your attention back to your spine, and follow the light down the spine into the ribs, and into the bones of the pelvis and then into the bones of the leg and the knee, the lower leg, the ankle and the feet and the toes.

☆ Allow that light to flow back up the skin of the body, around the toes, feet, calves and thighs, then the back and front of the abdomen, the back and front of the chest, and down the skin of the arms and into the hands and the tips of the fingers. Then let the light flow into the skin of your neck and up into the face and the back of the head, along the sides, into the ears and then to the top of head.

☆ Now imagine the light flowing under the skin and into all the muscles of the body. See or sense it flowing into the scalp, the muscles of the face, neck and shoulders, the upper arms, the lower arms, and down into the hands and fingers. The light then travels into the muscles of the back, the chest and abdomen and buttocks, and into the muscles of the legs and calves and feet.

☆ Now allow the light to flow through your circulation system, back through all the blood and drainage vessels, all the way back up the body, through your legs, your abdomen, into the heart. From the heart follow the light into the lungs, the arms and neck, and back into the head, face and scalp and towards the brain. Let the light flow into the brain, and feel the different parts of the brain: the areas for seeing, hearing, speaking, feeling, tasting, touching, smelling, moving; the areas for communication and the association of ideas; and the areas that allow you to co-ordinate, keep breathing, digesting, circulating the blood, the areas that control the rest of the body.

☆ Now let the light flow down the spinal cord and through the nervous system, through all the nerves that light up the body with the brain's messages. Let the light flow into the nerves all over your body, into the arms, chest, abdomen and legs, and then imagine the light from all these areas flowing out to fill your aura, the energy body that surrounds you. Sense the energy from your auric field flowing back from the energy body, back inside, flowing in through the eyes to let you see, the ears to hear, the mouth to breathe and taste, and filling the lungs. Feel this energy pouring down into the stomach and intestines and liver, the pancreas, the gall bladder and the spleen, finally flowing into the kidneys and down into the bladder and out of the body.

☆ Now feel the healing effects of the white light on your body; in particular, if any areas are more difficult to visu-alise, or seem red or orange in colour, you may like to bathe them in blue light and concentrate on them. You may be guided to certain areas of 'stored' emotions, so concentrate on the feelings in these areas. Ask them what is 'stored' there, and notice the words or the shape or colour of the feeling. If it feels safe, visualise these images slowly melting and being carried off by the light to be neutralised by the Universe or the Divine, and then replaced by healing, positive light. Gradually allow your entire body to be soothed and relaxed.

☆ When you've finished, imagine your whole body wrapped in white light. End the visualisation by returning to the room in which you are sitting or lying, slowly letting your awareness return. Open your eyes and feel relaxed, yet fully awake and alert.

8

Treating Others
With Reiki

Treating other people with Reiki is a very pleasurable experience. In most cases it feels almost as good as receiving the Reiki yourself. Much satisfaction is gained in being able to help people, and the majority of Reiki students enjoy treating their friends and family, and find that is enough. Some students, however, are keen to become Reiki practitioners, either to add to other therapies in which they are already qualified, or in order to make a living. If this is the case, obviously you need plenty of practice on willing volunteers, and I would always recommend that you take a Second Degree course so that you are able to use a greater range of techniques (see Chapter 6). Throughout this chapter I use the terms 'practitioner and client' for ease, but I actually refer to any person using Reiki to treat anyone other than themselves.

Whether you are working as a practitioner or simply offering Reiki to a friend, it is always necessary to be respectful of your client's needs. Even when treating people you know well, you have the same responsibility to ensure that they feel comfortable, safe and supported and can rely on your confidentiality.

Reiki Treatments

Most people's first contact with Reiki is through receiving a Reiki treatment, which takes about an hour and is carried out with the client remaining fully clothed (except for shoes) and tucked up comfortably with a blanket and pillows, usually on a therapy couch. The practitioner's hands are placed on the body and kept still for a few minutes in each place (see the hand position diagrams on pages 118–19). The client usually feels very relaxed and peaceful as the energy flows through their body, although occasionally they might feel emotional as old patterns surface. Tell them there may be a 'healing crisis' – temporary physical symptoms, such as a sudden cold – in the days immediately following a treatment, as the energy works through the blockages and the body does its best to get rid of them. The client may also experience a shift in consciousness, a realisation of the causes of the problems. This is an important part of healing, and if the client wants to talk about it they should be encouraged to do so. However, remember that your client is entitled to expect your complete confidentiality, so never talk to others about particular clients or their treatments.

What Can be Treated?

Most people coming for a Reiki treatment want help with specific physical problems, ranging from frequent headaches or frozen shoulders to more serious complaints such as chronic pain or cancer. Some simply want to be able to relax and cope better with the stresses of modern life. The potential with Reiki is unlimited, so anything can be treated, but it is important to rid yourself of specific expectations of what it will do, and how fast it will perform. Many physical symptoms are eased very quickly, while others may need more Reiki before starting to respond, but it is your own body that is actually doing the healing. Some people report amazing, even miraculous, effects, but remember that 'healing' is not always the same as 'curing'. Healing doesn't always occur on the physical level first. Because Reiki works holistically and is guided by the God-consciousness it may be that healing needs to happen first at the emotional level, with the releasing of anger, guilt or hatred. Healing may be required first at the mental level, releasing negative thoughts, concepts or attitudes, before the physical symptom can be addressed.

It is particularly important to rid yourself of expectations of the results of a Reiki treatment if the client has been diagnosed as terminally ill. Occasionally miracles do happen with Reiki, and the person recovers completely, or goes into substantial remission, but it cannot be expected every time. We do not decide how Reiki will affect the person we are treating. In the case of someone who is dying it may be that it will simply help them to make their transition more peacefully. It can be a very beautiful and rewarding experience to help someone towards their death, knowing that by being a channel for Reiki we have helped to alleviate the pain and distress of that person's final days or weeks.

Who Can be Treated?

Reiki is suitable for absolutely anyone. Babies and small children love Reiki, although they don't often want to stay still long enough for a full treatment, and since they are so much smaller than an adult they don't need as much anyway. It is far easier to treat them casually, allowing the Reiki to flow while you hold them or as they sit on your knee. Older children and teenagers seem either wildly enthusiastic, or rather suspicious, but once they have the opportunity to receive some, they usually like it. Pregnant women often find Reiki to be very soothing for themselves and their unborn child, and it can be really beneficial to both mother and baby to give Reiki during the birth process. Elderly people also find it very helpful with all the aches and pains which old age seems to bring.

CASE HISTORIES

In the following examples people who have been treated either by myself or by some of my students, indicate the wide range of ailments which can be helped by Reiki. Most of these cases were of hands-on healing, but I have also included a few which were successful as a result of distant healing using Second Degree techniques (see Chapter 6).

☆ A woman had a painful frozen shoulder for which she had been receiving physiotherapy for several months. After some 40 minutes of Reiki, applied directly to the shoulder, the pain had gone and she had completely normal movement of the arm once more.

☆ After giving a talk about Reiki I was approached by a woman who told me her elderly mother was in too much pain with spondylitis to come indoors, so she was sitting in her car outside the hall. I sat behind her with my hands on her neck for nearly an hour. When I took my hands away she turned her head to thank me, saying she felt much better. Her daughter promptly burst into tears, as her mother had been unable to turn her head for several years!

☆ One of my students treated her friend who was about to undergo surgery for a badly prolapsed uterus. While treating the area over the uterus the student felt tremendous heat in her hands, but, more unusually, felt movement under her hands which puzzled and slightly alarmed her. A few days later her friend went for a final check-up with the consultant, who became quite agitated upon examining her again, constantly referring to notes from the previous hospital visit. These had indicated that the prolapse was serious enough for surgery to be the only option, but it appeared that the uterus had returned to normal. The consultant could find no explanation, but her patient said, 'It's the Reiki!'.

☆ A young woman with gynaecological problems was examined in hospital. An endoscopy and an operation to remove a cyst revealed that her fallopian tubes were so badly damaged that she would never be able to have children. After several weeks of daily distant Reiki treatments her partner paid for her to have another examination at a different hospital. The endoscopy showed that her fallopian tubes were perfectly healthy, and there was no scar tissue to suggest the removal of a cyst – it had healed.

☆ Frequent migraines that, after a single treatment, have not returned five years later.

☆ Vaginal polyps which disappeared after three treatments.

☆ Serious long-term diarrhoea that was halted with a consequent return of normal bowel movement after one treatment.

☆ Long-term pain down one side of the body, resulting from a car accident, was relieved for the first time in six years after only one treatment.

☆ Increased energy returning with regular treatments after several years of ME (chronic fatigue syndrome).

☆ Post-operative distant Reiki given after triple heart by-pass surgery accelerated the healing so that there was virtually no scarring.

☆ Assorted complaints: headaches, backaches, stiff necks, knee problems, ankle problems, stomach-aches, pulled muscles, inflammation, insomnia.

If Physical Healing Fails to Happen

Not everyone wants to be healed. On a conscious level you would expect everybody would choose to be healed into good health, but our motivations are often subconscious. Many people have a considerable investment in their own ill-health, for various reasons. Since childhood they may have found that the only time they get any attention is when they are ill, or that they get treated differently when they are sick, or that being ill means they don't have to face up to something that is going on in their lives.

A young man came for treatments for epilepsy. Quite quickly the frequency of the epileptic fits was reduced to about 20 per cent of what it had been before, but then he stopped making progress. Eventually, with some coaxing, he admitted that he didn't really want to get rid of the epilepsy because it made him feel special. Once he had admitted this we were able to work out a programme to raise his self-esteem so that he could feel good without the epilepsy.

This case is not as unusual as it may sound. Each of us is a unique individual, experiencing life in a unique way, so it is hardly surprising that we have complex and sometimes baffling responses to things such as illness. Some people try really hard to heal themselves, using all the self-help techniques available, and they are often puzzled and upset when their efforts aren't immediately successful. Often this occurs because the causative levels are very deeply buried, and need to surface layer by layer to be understood, so the healing takes time. Sometimes the illness itself is the lesson which has to be learned, perhaps something that affects the mobility of the person, bringing them literally to a full stop so that they are forced to look inside and pursue insight and self-awareness. At other times they are trying too hard. They are so busy 'doing' things about their illness that they've forgotten how to 'be'. They may simply need to acknowledge the illness and its effects on them, reaching a level of acceptance of what it is like in the present. In trying desperately to rid themselves of physical symptoms they may have actually blocked any real understanding of the lesson the illness was trying to teach them. Whatever happens, it is important not to be self-critical or to blame the body for not co-operating. Use Reiki on the situation, and look within for guidance on what would be the best way to progress.

How Many Treatments?

This is rather like asking 'How long is a piece of string?' The answer clearly depends upon what is being treated. For minor health problems or to alleviate stress and encourage relaxation, one or two treatments may be enough, while major illnesses are likely to require many treatments. For very serious or chronic conditions it is generally accepted that four treatments, preferably on consecutive days, form an extremely effective way to start any treatment programme, allowing each of the four energy bodies to become balanced. If it isn't possible to do the treatments on consecutive days, then at least two per week would be ideal.

When dealing with serious illness it is recommended to give a full treatment to the affected person every day for at least 21 days. This is obviously easier to achieve if it involves a member of your own family or a friend who lives locally, but in other cases a combination of 'hands-on' and distant treatments can be given. (The techniques taught at Second Degree allow you to give a proper full treatment at a distance with exactly the same effects as if the person was with you.) In all other instances, you simply need to follow your inner guidance and do what feels right.

Incidentally don't feel you should only give Reiki treatments to people who are physically ill. Reiki is beneficial at any time, encouraging deep relaxation and a feeling of peace and tranquillity. In today's high-stress climate, it is precious. Ideally, even if you give yourself a self-treatment every day, it's a good idea to receive a full treatment at least once a month to help promote health.

Equipment

Reiki can be used without any equipment at all. All you really need is a pair of hands! However, if you want to carry out treatments it is sensible to have a suitable therapy couch, together with several pillows, pillow cases, fitted sheets and a soft blanket. Several types of therapy couch are on the market, varying in price from £100–350 for portable couches, some of which have legs of adjustable height, up to several thousand pounds for hydraulically operated static couches. You probably won't need to invest in an expensive couch until you have taken Reiki Second Degree, the level recommended if you want to set up as a Reiki practitioner. In the meantime there are various ways of carrying out treatments using other inexpensive alternatives.

A dining table is usually about the right height. If it is sturdy enough (some people can be pretty heavy!) and long enough, you could place some thick foam on top (a Z-bed mattress is ideal) and cover it with a sheet. Another alternative could be a heavy-duty pasting table with foam on top – it must be a heavy-duty model made of stronger materials, and with wooden braces that can be screwed into place to make the whole thing solid, because ordinary pasting tables are definitely not suitable!

Another alternative, if you're reasonably agile, is to do treatments with a person lying on a camp bed or sun lounger with you sitting on the floor with your legs under the bed (although you may find sitting on a cushion more comfortable). It is also possible to do treatments with people lying on the floor or on a conventional divan bed, but this can be mightily uncomfortable for the practitioner after the first ten minutes or so.

Preparing To Give a Treatment

If you are going to give someone a full Reiki treatment, it is important that they should come into a comfortable, safe and supportive environment. They need you to behave in a professional manner, even if they know you really well. The room should be clean and tidy. You can also cleanse it with Reiki by sitting quietly for a few moments, allowing Reiki to flow through your hands and out into the room, intending that it should cleanse the space of any negative energies. Set up the therapy couch if you have one, and place the clean pillows and blanket ready, perhaps burning incense or essential oils to fill the room with a pleasant smell. (Some people are sensitive to certain smells, so check first.) Ensure the room is at an appropriate temperature, and that there will be no interruptions from telephones, children, pets or other distractions. You should also take off your watch and any metal jewellery, and wash your hands before giving a treatment.

Many people are quite nervous before having their first Reiki treatment, so always make a little time beforehand to talk to them. They usually find it reassuring when they realise that they can remain fully clothed except for shoes, and you can also spend some time describing the hand positions so that they know exactly what to expect. Tell them about the experiences they may have, such as warmth or tingling where the hands are placed or the possibility of feeling rather emotional or having vivid dreams. Discuss with the client the reason they have come for a treatment, and give them a chance to ask questions. It can also be helpful to ask them to allow their minds to release all thoughts and fears so they can focus fully on the present experience.

The person receiving Reiki should take off his or her shoes, watch, spectacles and any metal jewellery. Otherwise they should be fully clothed. One pillow should be placed under the neck and another under the knees when the person is lying on their back. That pillow should be moved to beneath the ankles when the client is lying on their front. Sometimes a soft blanket over the client makes them feel nurtured and more relaxed.

Both practitioner and client should relax and enjoy the treatment, so before you start make sure that both of you are comfortable, that the therapy couch is at a comfortable height for use and the client is warm enough. Talking or asking questions during the treatment is an individual matter, but quiet surroundings allow the client to relax more thoroughly, so simply playing soft, relaxing music is often best.

Traditional Hand Positions for the Treatment of Others

To give a full treatment, there are 12 hand positions on the head and body that are normally held for five minutes, with the option of leaving the hands longer on any position where a lot of Reiki is still flowing to indicate that area needs more. The whole treatment should take about an hour, so it is very important that both you and your client are comfortable. Holding the hands still for any length of time can be a strain if you don't have the Reiki couch at the right height, or if you haven't placed a chair in the right position. The treatment usually starts with the client lying on his or her back, with the practitioner standing or sitting behind the head for the first five hand positions. The practitioner's hands rest gently on the person's body; be careful not to exert any pressure.

Note that it is possible to hold the hands just above the body in each of the hand positions. This can be useful if there is some form of injury where even the lightest pressure might be painful.

Be very gentle as the hands are moved from one position to another. It is preferable to move one hand at a time so that you have continuity of contact with the person. For hand positions 6–8 (see page 118), you will need to stand or sit at the side of the person being treated (either side is fine). When you finish treating the front of the body you need to gently rouse the client (who is usually deeply relaxed at this stage) and ask them to turn over on to the front. Make sure they are comfortable and help them to turn over if necessary, adjusting the pillows so that the head rests comfortably. Place the other pillow under the ankles to take the strain off the back.

When the client is settled, the treatment continues. It is easiest to perform hand position 9, on the shoulders, from behind the head, although an alternative is to place both hands on one shoulder for five minutes, and then to move both hands to the other shoulder for another five minutes. This is especially good for people who hold a lot of tension in their shoulders. You then progress down one side of the body (it doesn't matter which side) for hand positions 10–12.

If the person is unable to lie on their stomach – for example, a pregnant woman – they can lie on their side instead. It is then more comfortable for you to sit at the side of the therapy couch to carry out the rest of the treatment. If the client cannot lie down, then the treatment can fairly easily be carried out with them sitting in a chair. You can stand or sit behind them for the head positions, and then sit at their side for the hand positions on the front of the body. If they sit on a dining chair, then the hand positions for the back of the body are also relatively easy. If they can only sit in an armchair and are unable to lean forward a little, you can either spend extra time on the front of the body, or place your hands on the back of the chair in places which roughly correspond to the hand positions for the back of the body. Reiki can easily go through the back of a chair.

Hand Positions for the Front and Back of the Body

Front of Body

From behind the head:

1 One hand cupped over each eye (fingertips *not* touching cheek).

2 One hand cupped just above each ear (fingertips level with each earlobe).
3 Both hands cradling the back of the head.
4 One hand on each side of the neck (about 20cm away from the neck).
5 Hands in a V-shape at the top of the chest.

From either side:
6 One hand in front of the other at the solar plexus (midriff area).
7 One hand in front of the other at waist level.
8 Hands in a V-shape at the pelvic area, pointing diagonally downwards.

Back of Body
From behind the head:
9 One hand on each shoulder *or* **9A** both hands on one shoulder *and* **9B** both hands on the other shoulder.

From either side:
10 One hand in front of the other on either side of back.
11 One hand in front of the other at waist level.
12 One hand on each buttock.

Additional Hand Positions

Because Reiki always flows to the areas of the physical body or energy bodies which need it, and because the traditional 12 hand positions enable the Reiki to flow easily and effectively into all the major chakra points, other hand positions are not really necessary. However, over the years many other hand positions have been used, and the commonest additional positions taught are those on the legs and feet.

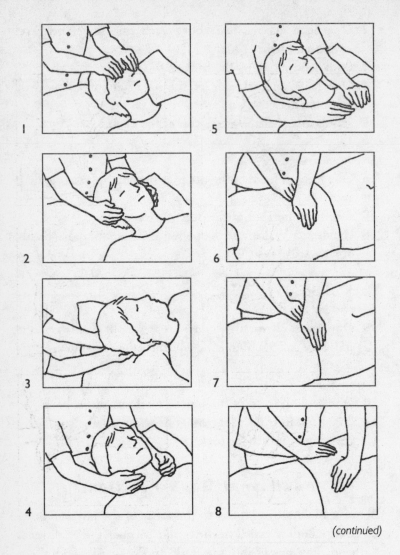

(continued)

Traditional Reiki hand positions for treating others.

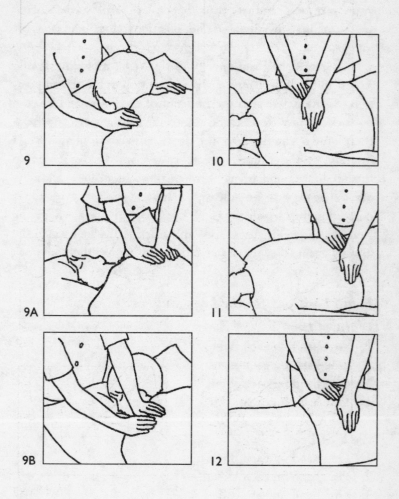

9

9A

9B

10

11

12

These are usually held for about two minutes, but again use your intuition and if your hands are still experiencing sensation in a particular hand position, then continue for longer.

We 'store' blocked energy in our legs, including family issues, difficult decisions and our direction in life. Hand positions 8 (the pelvic area on the front of the body) and 12 (the buttocks) allow Reiki to flow into the Base chakra and from there down the legs to the feet. However, giving Reiki directly to the thighs, knees, calves and ankles helps to further loosen and break through these blockages, allowing the old energy to be released. The feet have energy zones corresponding to all parts of the physical body, so giving Reiki to the heels, toes, tops and soles of the feet sends the healing again to every organ and system within the body.

Hand Positions for the Legs and Feet

Front of Legs
1 One hand on each thigh.
2 One hand on each knee.
3 One hand on each shin.
4 One hand on each ankle.

Back of Legs
1 One hand on each thigh.
2 One hand on each knee.
3 One hand on each calf.
4 One hand on each heel.

The Feet (first one, then the other)
1 (& 5) One hand either side of ankle (if not treated at 4 under Front of Legs).

2 (& 6)   One hand above, one below the foot.
3 (& 7)   One hand above, one below the toes.
4   One hand under sole of each foot.

If the client has a health problem in a particular part (or parts) of the body, it makes sense to devote additional time to those areas or to add a hand position if required. No specific hand positions are given for the upper arms, elbows, forearms, wrists, hands or fingers, because Reiki flows down the arms particularly when using the hand positions on the upper chest and shoulders — but if there is a health problem there, please treat it!

Use the 12 hand positions of the traditional full treatment as a framework. In most cases that will be all you need. However, if you really feel it is necessary, add to them. Don't be afraid to be creative. Reiki is a dynamic energy and a living healing system, so use it in ways which feel right to you.

Reiki Treatment Using Second Degree Symbols

If you have taken a Reiki Second Degree course then the hand positions for a full treatment remain the same, but you can reduce the time in each position to between two and a half and three minutes because you can use the Reiki symbols that intensify the flow of energy throughout the treatment. Other additional techniques taught at Second Degree level can also enhance a Reiki treatment, such as using the Mental Symbol to promote deep mental and emotional healing.

After the Treatment

At the end of the treatment it is pleasant (but not essential) to smooth the client's aura. Hold both your hands at least 6–8 inches (15–20cm) above the body. Starting above the crown of the head, allow your hands to flow gently over the body (keeping 15–20cm away) right down to below the soles of the feet. (Always do it from head down to feet, as doing it in the opposite direction can be quite disturbing.) Repeat this three times, and then gently rouse the client by touching their shoulder and saying their name softly. Try not to hurry the person, but if the client is having difficulty in 'coming round', then gently massage their feet

When they are ready, help them to sit up, and offer them a glass of water. Please advise them to drink plenty of water for the next few days to help the body to flush out the toxins which may have been dislodged by the Reiki. Some people feel energised immediately after a treatment, while others feel sleepy and incredibly peaceful. If the person seems at all 'spaced out', then make sure you ground them by getting them to sit with their feet flat on the floor. Take your hands and place one on each of the client's feet, and visualise the energy flowing out through the soles of the feet into the earth below. It is amazing how quickly people return to feeling normal after this simple exercise.

Confidentiality and Ethics

Your clients should be able to rely totally on your confidentiality, as you are in a privileged position when treating them. They will probably regard you as a medical professional – which you are not, unless you are medically trained – and will listen carefully to anything you say. You may feel it necessary to advise someone to have further treatment(s) to maintain wellness, but on no account should you attempt to diagnose any illnesses. If you feel there is a serious problem, you should gently advise the person to seek medical help in addition to Reiki, but do so in a way that will not alarm them. You may sometimes wish to encourage a client to examine their life-style and make positive, healthy modifications, but this should always be done with the utmost sensitivity and in a positive, helpful manner, without criticism.

It is equally important not to promise any particular outcome from a treatment. The person's higher self decides the amount of healing required, and a higher consciousness directs the Reiki to those areas of greatest need, so you are little more than a channel for the energy. Promising miracle cures is both unethical and dangerous, because you could be falsely raising hopes. Miracles do happen, but no one knows when.

Another matter to consider is whether you should offer Reiki or wait to be asked. Obviously people need to know first that you practise Reiki, so it is fine to talk about it. However, if you always offer Reiki rather than waiting to be asked, people could feel obliged to say 'yes', and then you would effectively be interfering in their healing. I usually tackle this by explaining what Reiki is, stressing that I would be happy to demonstrate it or to treat them, but that I don't want to put them under any pressure, and I then wait to be asked.

Reiki as First Aid

Giving a full treatment is clearly not the only way to give Reiki, so please don't feel constrained by the idea that you always need a therapy couch and time to do 12 hand positions! If anyone around you needs help, you have a tool available for which you only need your hands. Many minor problems or injuries such as headaches, toothache, muscle strain, cramp, cuts and bruises can quickly be alleviated with Reiki. Simply place your hands on the affected area and allow the Reiki to flow. In my experience most aches and pains will ease within a few minutes, and will often disappear completely within a quarter of an hour. There's no specific amount of time for such events. Allow your inner guidance to let you know when the Reiki has stopped flowing. Usually this will mean that you no longer feel any sensation in your hands, but for those people who get very little sensation anyway it may surprise you, but you will still 'know' when it is right to take your hands away.

Combining Reiki with Other Complementary Therapies

Reiki works well with most complementary therapies, but particularly with any 'hands-on' therapy such as aromatherapy, reflexology, shiatsu, chiropractic, osteopathy or any others involving massage or manipulation. If the therapist is attuned to Reiki, the energy automatically flows from the therapist's hands during the session if the client needs it. The client's higher self or inner wisdom decides how much Reiki they need, and the Rei, or God-consciousness decides where the Reiki goes, so at this level the practitioner only needs to be willing to let the energy flow.

I know many reflexologists who specifically use Reiki at the end of the reflexology treatment, placing their palms on the client's feet and allowing the Reiki to flow around the whole energy system as a deeply relaxing finale. Another student who was an aromatherapist eventually called her practice 'Aroma-Reiki', because so much Reiki flowed into her clients when she was giving them an aromatherapy massage!

For therapies involving the consumption of any internal preparation, such as homoeopathy, Bach flower remedies or herbal medicine, the bottle or container can be held in the hands to allow Reiki to flow into the medication. In doing this, it is usual to have the intention that Reiki should flow into the remedy. The easiest way is to say to yourself (silently or aloud): 'Let Reiki flow into this remedy to enhance its effectiveness for the highest possible good.'

Reiki is always given for the highest possible good, and this effectively releases the practitioner from any particular expectations of, or responsibility for, what the Reiki will do.

The Balance Between Reiki and Conventional Medicine

Some people seem to think that complementary and conventional medicine don't mix, but this is not the case. Many health professionals are taking an increasing interest in complementary medicine. I have trained numerous nurses, physio-therapists, occupational therapists, doctors and even a consultant in Reiki. Increasing numbers of hospitals, hospices, clinics and doctors' surgeries now feature healing and other forms of complementary therapies in their range of services.

If you wish to carry out Reiki healing in any of these environments, however, they usually require you to have qualifications in anatomy and physiology. In order to use Reiki we don't need to know anything about the body, because the Reiki is always guided by a subtle wisdom to those parts which need it, but that can be a difficult concept to explain to a medical professional who has spent many years acquiring knowledge and qualifications. I suggest that it is far better to gain the extra knowledge and then put your abilities to good use if this is something you really want to do. You will also need to carry public liability insurance, which is normal for therapists anyway.

There are some general guidelines to follow when using Reiki with someone receiving conventional medical treatment:

☆ *Never* advise anyone to stop taking any medicines or to stop seeing their doctor or other health professional.

☆ *Never* try to diagnose what is wrong with anyone (unless you are a doctor).

☆ *Always* advise them to check with their doctor, if they wish, that receiving Reiki healing is OK. (We know that Reiki always works for the highest good, but this can provide reassurance.)

☆ Also, *always* advise them to see a doctor if their health problem does not respond to treatment, or if you intuitively feel there may be some underlying serious problem. (This must only be done with tact and sensitivity, as you do not wish to disturb them, and it is not your place to diagnose.)

As with complementary therapies, any medication can be held in the hands and given Reiki to enhance its beneficial effects and decrease any side effects. Giving Reiki to someone after any surgical operation can dramatically increase the rate at which the wounds heal and also reduce scarring. The same is true of giving Reiki to broken bones.

One school of thought within the Reiki community says that Reiki should not be sent to someone by distant healing while they are having an operation or when they are receiving chemotherapy, as one of the effects of Reiki is to rid the body of toxins. Obviously in these cases the toxins – the anaesthetic or the strong drugs – are meant to benefit the patient. However, I believe that Reiki can never do harm, and always works for the highest good, and I have always found Reiki to be beneficial in these instances. My trust in Reiki is such that I sent distant healing to my daughter during an operation, and felt only the most wonderful, peaceful connection with her. Afterwards she came round more quickly and easily than usual, and couldn't wait to get out of hospital. I know of many cases where Reiki has been given very successfully to people receiving chemotherapy and radiation treatment, and their recovery rate has been excellent, with virtually no side effects. However, always trust your intuition in such circumstances. If it feels right, do it. If it doesn't, then don't!

One slight word of caution is offered for the treatment of broken bones or injuries where a part of the body, such as the end of a finger, has been cut off. Because Reiki accelerates the body's own ability to heal, sometimes with quite dramatic results, it may be best to wait until after the bone has been set if it is a bad break, or until after the end of the finger has been reattached surgically, before treating the affected part. To relieve shock and pain in such circumstances, Reiki can be given to any other part of the body (the Heart chakra, Solar Plexus chakra or adrenals are particularly good for this purpose). The Reiki will then flow around the whole body, but not be so concentrated at the point of injury. After medical intervention, however, Reiki away as much as you like!

However, I also know of amazing cases where broken bones have been healed completely with Reiki within a matter of hours. Serious injuries have healed beautifully with virtually no scarring. Again, use your intuition, and trust Reiki to work for the highest good.

Group Treatments With Reiki

In Dr Hayashi's clinic in Japan it was common to have several practitioners treating each person. While that is very unusual today, it is a really good idea to get together with other people who practice Reiki to have a 'Reiki sharing' where you swap treatments. To have two, four, six or even more people treating you at once is a lovely experience. The largest number I have ever received a treatment from is 14. It was quite blissful! The more people you have treating you, the less time it takes, as you simply share the hand positions out between you, usually with each person working down one side of the body only. With many people you can cover all of the body, and the legs, feet, arms and hands as well.

Finding a Reiki Practitioner

If you haven't already experienced a Reiki treatment, you will probably want to find a suitable practitioner. The Useful Addresses section may be helpful, but you can also try your local complementary health clinic, health food shops or 'new age' shops which have noticeboards where therapists place business cards. One of the best ways of finding a good practitioner is to ask people you know to recommend someone.

9

Being Creative With Reiki

Throughout this book I have stressed that the potential with Reiki is unlimited. It isn't just for your own self-healing, or for the healing of other people, but can be used creatively in many different ways. The only limitation is your own imagination. I hope these suggestions spark even more of your own ideas. Use Reiki as much as possible to foster healing, harmony and balance in the world around you.

Sending Reiki Through the Aura

At times it isn't possible to treat someone by laying your hands on them, as at the scene of an accident, or to soothe a crying child or an agitated animal. In these cases it is perfectly acceptable to send the Reiki through the aura. Imagine your aura expanding until it encompasses the person or animal to whom you wish to give Reiki, and then mentally 'switch on' the Reiki by intending that it should flow. If you wish, hold your hands out in the general direction of the recipient (although this isn't strictly necessary). If the person or animal is accepting of the Reiki, you will start to feel it flowing from your hands; if not, then nothing will happen. I have found this method particularly useful for soothing crying or distressed children in crowded restaurants when I have wanted to enjoy a quiet meal!

Treating Animals, Birds, Reptiles or Fish

Most types of animal respond very well to Reiki. My experience has been limited to household pets and occasionally farm animals, but other Reiki healers who have tried their skill on a wider variety have enjoyed successful results.

Animals seem to be much more in tune with their own health and energy needs than humans, so while some will happily sit or stand for a long time to receive Reiki, others will quickly move away. Pets who would usually sit happily to be stroked may walk off if you try to give them Reiki. A student who attended the second day of a Reiki First Degree course with her arms and hands covered in scratches admitted she had been so enthusiastic after the first day that she was determined to give her cat some Reiki, so she had chased it all around the house in order to try out her new skill. Unfortunately the cat made its own decision painfully obvious!

As a general rule there are no specific hand positions for animals. It largely depends upon where you can reach and where the animal will allow you to touch. Reiki will flow around the whole body even if you can only place your hands in one position. Some animals seem to dislike Reiki being given directly on to their spine, although cats can be an exception to this. If you should ever need to give Reiki to an animal which might prove dangerous, then it is perfectly acceptable to send the Reiki through your own aura into the auric field of the animal. This is also the way to treat an animal that won't let you come close, either because it is too nervous or because it is not domesticated.

Farm animals such as cattle, sheep or pigs are often best treated through the aura from the edge of the field or beside the pen, or with the Second Degree distant treatment. Horses are generally easier to deal with as they are more used to human contact, so you could place your hands on their head and then work down one side of the body and then the other. Cats and dogs are also fairly easy to treat, and will normally stay still for as long as the Reiki is required. Depending upon the size of the animal, one hand position on the head and two or three down the body should be sufficient. Smaller mammals such as rabbits, hamsters or gerbils can just be held in the hands so that the Reiki can flow into them. This same technique is suitable for smaller reptiles, unless they are likely to bite, in which case you can hold your hands on either side of the tank in which they live. Large reptiles or snakes are also best left in their tanks or other living environments, as are coldwater or tropical fish, or insects such as crickets or spiders. Pet birds can be treated by placing your hands on either side of their cage, or by holding them in your hands. Wild birds or other small wild animals are probably best placed in a cardboard box with air holes before being treated, as contact with humans can be very frightening. The shock can even cause them to die in some cases.

If there is a specific injury then that is where treatment should be concentrated, but take care not to directly touch any part which might cause the animal pain. The amount of time required will vary greatly and depend upon the size of the animal. A large dog such as a German Shepherd will take more Reiki than a smaller breed like a dachshund. Small mammals, birds, reptiles and fish will usually need treating for only a few minutes. If in doubt, leave your hands in place until you feel the energy 'switch off', but please use your own intuition and go with whatever feels right.

Another way to help animals is to Reiki their food and water to enhance its nutritional qualities and offset adverse effects of chemicals or preservatives. Any homoeopathic remedies or medication dispensed by a veterinary surgeon can also be given Reiki to help to offset any possible side effects.

Using Reiki With Plants and Seeds

Seeds and plants respond extremely well to being treated with Reiki, and I have tested this out many times. I have kept houseplants alive for months without water – even 'difficult' plants like poinsettias – just by giving them Reiki each day. I have also tried planting seeds in identical compost and containers and given Reiki to only half the seeds. In each case those given Reiki grew faster and more strongly than those which were not treated, and also had a 100 per cent germination rate.

To give Reiki to seeds, simply hold the packet between your hands and intend that Reiki should flow to the seeds. Alternatively, plant them and then hold your hands over the seed trays. For houseplants the easiest way is to hold your hands either on each side of the pot or about six inches (15cm) away from the plant for about a minute. If you have many plants, a quick and easy idea is to Reiki the water for their regular watering. This is even possible when watering a garden using a hosepipe; as the water passes through the section of the pipe you are holding, it can receive Reiki.

Reiki and Inanimate Objects

It may stretch your credulity, but Reiki can work very well on inanimate objects like cars, computers and washing machines. This isn't really as strange as it may sound. Everything in the universe is energy, and all 'man-made' objects start out as natural materials. Those natural materials may have changed state, but they are still energy. I have succeeded in getting computers, dishwashers, vacuum cleaners and cars to work after they had broken down. I'm not suggesting that Reiki should be used in place of proper maintenance – your car will still need a regular service – but it certainly can be useful when things go wrong!

Reiki with Food and Drink

It makes good sense to give Reiki to all the food you eat and to everything you drink. Not only does it enhance the nutritional value of the food, but it can help to balance the ill effects of additives and chemicals and bring the food into harmony with your body. I personally like to use Reiki as a type of blessing. It feels good to exchange some energy with our food, because everything we eat was once a living thing, not just meat or fish. Vegetables, fruit, nuts and seeds are also alive, if not in the same way, but they too have given up a form of life to provide us with energy so that we may continue to live.

In line with the Reiki principle 'Show gratitude to every living thing', be grateful for what you eat. You don't have to hold your hands over your food in an overt act. You can be discreet and hold your hands at the sides of your plate, or around the cup or glass just for a minute. You might like to say a prayer of thanks either silently or out loud. The one I use is: 'I give Reiki to this food/drink in grateful thanks to the earth, the plants, the animals and the people who have helped to bring this nourishment to me. I also give Reiki to this food/drink to enhance its nutritional quality, and to bring it into harmony with my body so that it helps me to be healthy and fit.'

Using Reiki With Crystals

You can use Reiki to cleanse any type of crystal, simply by holding the crystal in your hands and intending that the Reiki should cleanse it. It is also possible to programme crystals with Reiki so that they carry the healing energy. I have found clear quartz, rose quartz and amethyst are the best for this purpose. Hold the cleansed crystal in your hands and allow Reiki to flow into it, and 'programme' the crystal by intending that it should hold the healing energy, and then release it when required. You can then carry the crystal around with you to aid your own healing, or give it to someone else who needs healing energy.

You can also write down any problem you are experiencing on a piece of paper and place it under the crystal, intending that the Reiki flow constantly into the problem to create healing for the highest possible good. It is best to cleanse the crystal and reprogramme it once a week to maintain the strength of the energy. Try holding your hand over a quartz crystal before programming it with Reiki, and then again afterwards. You will be amazed at the power coming from the crystal after it has been filled with Reiki. There will usually be enough to make your hand tingle.

Distant or Absent Reiki

To carry out distant healing effectively with Reiki you really need the techniques taught at Second Degree level. They enable you to send very powerful healing to anyone, anywhere, at any time (including the past and the future). These techniques also allow you to carry out a complete Reiki treatment on someone at a distance with the same effectiveness as if they were receiving hands-on treatment. It is possible to send some healing at First Degree level, although it won't be as strong. As a simile, I usually describe distant healing at Second Degree level as like a laser beam, where there is no diminution of strength regardless of distance, whereas First Degree is more like a normal torch beam, which spreads out and loses light the further it goes.

If you want to send healing and love to people, just write their names on a piece of paper and hold it in your hands, intending that Reiki should go to them. You can also use a photograph in the same way.

Using Reiki on Personal Problems and Situations

Whatever the problems, from strained relationships with your partner or family, to difficulties at work or with studying, you can use Reiki to help to permeate the situation with healing. Simply write the details down on paper – whether this takes a single sentence or several paragraphs – and then hold it between your hands, intending that Reiki should flow to the situation for the highest good. You really need to do this for at least ten minutes a day for as long as the situation exists, and you also need to detach yourself from specific expectations about the result. This can be difficult, because human nature wants a particular result! However Reiki always works for the highest good, and though we might believe we know what is best for us, we are not always right. You have to trust Reiki to bring you what you need, even if that isn't necessarily what you desire. Techniques taught at Second Degree level make working on problems and situations even more effective (see Chapter 6).

Empowering Affirmations and Goals

You can use a similar method for working on your goals and dreams with Reiki. Write down what you really want – a new job, a loving relationship, a cottage in the country – on a piece of paper. Be as specific as possible. Write down all the aspects of what you are seeking, so if you want a cottage in the country, specify the number of bedrooms and bathrooms, the type of kitchen, whether you want central heating or open fires, a small garden or acres of farmland, and so on. Then hold the paper in your hands and give it Reiki for at least ten minutes a day until you achieve what you want. But beware – be sure you want it before you ask for it! Your description needs to be very particular. Second Degree techniques empower this practice even more.

If you are working with affirmations – positive statements to help to reprogramme your thinking – then these can be made even more effective by writing them down and holding the paper in your hands, saying them over and over to yourself while giving them Reiki. This can be a really powerful method for change, so make sure that your affirmations are always really positive and fully in the present. For example, use 'I have a wonderful, loving relationship with a man/woman who loves me' even if this isn't the case right at this moment in time, rather than 'I will have . . .' or 'I would like . . .'

Earth Healing, World Situations and Disasters

The Earth really needs as much healing as we can give her. With Reiki you have a wonderful tool for planetary healing, and for sending healing to world situations or in crises or disasters. An organisation called Reiki Outreach International is dedicated to healing the planet and the human family (see page 139). There are many methods for Earth healing. Although all of them are enhanced by using Reiki, you could try some of the following suggestions even if you don't do Reiki. Simply use your thought energy and imagine white light going to the earth instead.

☆ Go to a place of power, such as an ancient stone circle. Either sit in the middle, or place your hands on one of the stones. Allow Reiki to flow into the stone and then around the circle, and into the earth itself.

☆ Sit or stand either outdoors or indoors with your palms facing downwards, and direct Reiki into the earth.

☆ Imagine that you are holding a small version of the world between your hands, and send it Reiki.

☆ Hold something in your hands to represent the earth, such as a stone, and fill it with Reiki, intending that the Reiki should fill the planet.

To send Reiki to situations such as famines, ecological disasters or war zones, write down the details of the situation and hold the piece of paper in your hands, intending that Reiki should go to it for the highest possible good. In this way the Reiki is not being constrained to go only to one aspect of the situation, such as the people affected by the famine, but to the whole, so that it can also permeate the aid agencies, the governments, any warring factions, and so on. It is gratifying to feel that you can do something to help, because so often we are too far removed from such situations to either fully understand them or to offer practical assistance.

The ideas listed above are just some of the ways in which Reiki can be used. There are many others. I'm sure that no one has yet discovered the full potential of Reiki. However, the more people use it, the more the mass consciousness will be raised, and the more we will be able to heal our beautiful planet.

Useful Addresses

The Reiki Association (UK), 2 Manor Cottages, Stockley Hill, Peterchurch, Hereford, HR2 0SS. Tel: 01981 550 829.
E-mail: reikiassoc_office@compuserve.com or reikiassoc_admin@compuserve.com
The phone line operates between 10 a.m. and 2 p.m. Monday to Friday. For a list of Reiki Masters, please send a cheque or postal order for £2.50 (payable to The Reiki Association) to the above address. For a list of Reiki practitioners in your area please telephone the above number.

The Reiki Association (Eire), 38 Waterpark Close, Carrigaline, County Cork, Eire.

Reiki Outreach International (UK contact), 17 Brincliffe Crescent, Sheffield, S11 9AW. Tel: 0114 255 2927.

The International Center for Reiki Training, 21421 Hilltop #28, Southfield, Michigan 48034, USA. Tel: 1-800-332-8112 or 248-948-8112. E-mail: reikicen@aol.com.
Website: http://www.reiki.org.

The Reiki Alliance, PO Box 41, Cataldo, Idaho 83810-1041, USA. Tel: 208 682-3535. Fax: 208-682-4848. E-mail: ReikiAlliance@compuserve.com

The Reiki Alliance (Europe), Postbus 75523, 1070 AM, Amsterdam, Netherlands. Tel: 00 31 20-6719276. Fax: 00 31 20-6711736. E-mail: 100125.466@compuserve.com

The Office of Grand Master, PO Box 220, Cataldo, Idaho 83810, USA. Tel: 208-682-9009. Fax: 208-682-9567. E-mail: grandmaster@nidlink.com. Website: http://www.furumoto.org

For details of Reiki courses, retreats and other workshops please send a stamped addressed envelope to Penelope Quest, c/o Libra, 8 Market Street, Kirkby Lonsdale, Cumbria, LA6 2AU or e-mail: pennyquest@yahoo.com

Further Reading

The following books are my recommendations from the many available on each subject, but do explore further. Though I have placed them under headings to make it easier to find the subjects you want to pursue, many of them cover topics which cross several categories.

Abundance Theory

Dyer, Wayne W., *Manifest Your Destiny,* Thorsons, 1998
Horan, Paula, *Abundance Through Reiki*, Lotus Light Publications, 1995
Roman, Sanaya and Packer, Duane, *Creating Money*, H. J. Kramer, 1988

Environmental Impact

Kingston, Karen, *Clear Your Clutter With Feng Shui*, Piatkus, 1998
Kingston, Karen, *Creating Sacred Space With Feng Shui,* Piatkus, 1996
Spear, William, *Feng Shui Made Easy*, Thorsons, 1995
Thurnell-Read, Jane, *Geopathic Stress*, Element, 1995

General Self-Help

Batmanghelidj, Dr F., *Your Body's Many Cries For Water*, The Therapist Ltd, 1997

Hartvic, Kirsten and Rowley, Dr Nic, *You Are What You Eat*, Piatkus, 1996

McDermott, Ian and O'Connor, Joseph, *NLP And Health*, Thorsons, 1996

Healing

Angelo, Jack, *Your Healing Power*, Piatkus, 1998

Brennan, Barbara Ann, *Hands Of Light*, Bantam Books, 1988

Brown, Dr Craig, *Optimum Healing*, Rider, 1998

Chopra, Deepak, M.D., *Quantum Healing*, Bantam Books, 1990

Gawain, Shakti, *The Four Levels of Healing*, Eden Grove Editions, 1997

Hay, Louise L., *You Can Heal Your Life*, Eden Grove Editions, 1988

Myss, Caroline, Ph.D., *Why People Don't Heal And How They Can*, Bantam Books, 1998

Siegel, Bernie S., M.D., *Love, Medicine and Miracles*, Arrow Books, 1988

Siegel, Bernie S., M.D., *Peace, Love and Healing*, Arrow Books, 1991

Metaphysical Causes of Disease

Dethlefsen, Thorwald and Dahlke, Rudiger, M.D., *The Healing Power of Illness*, Element, 1990

Hay, Louise L., *Heal Your Body*, Eden Grove Editions, 1989

Shapiro, Debbie, *Your Body Speaks Your Mind*, Piatkus, 1996

Metaphysical Living

Edwards, Gill, *Living Magically*, Piatkus, 1991

Edwards, Gill, *Stepping Into The Magic*, Piatkus, 1993

Gawain, Shakti, *Living In The Light*, Eden Grove Editions, 1988

Jeffers, Susan, *Feel The Fear And Do It Anyway*, Arrow Books, 1991

Roberts, Jane, *The Nature Of Personal Reality*, Amber-Allen Publishing, 1974

Roman, Sanaya, *Living With Joy*, H. J. Kramer, 1986

Scovel-Shinn, Florence, *The Game Of Life and How To Play It*, L. N. Fowler, 1993

Reiki

Brown, Fran, *Living Reiki — Takata's Teachings*, Life Rhythm, 1992

Horan, Paula, *Empowerment Through Reiki*, Lotus Light Publications, 1992

Petter, Frank Arjava, *Reiki Fire*, Lotus Light Publications, 1997

Rand, William L., *Reiki, the Healing Touch*, Vision Publications, 1991

Index

*Piatkus Guides, written by experts, combine background information with
practical exercises, and are designed to change the way you live.
Titles include:*

Tarot Cassandra Eason

Tarot's carefully graded advice enables readers to obtain
excellent readings from Day One. You will quickly gain a
thorough knowledge of both Major and Minor Arcanas and their
symbolism, and learn how to use a variety of Tarot spreads.

Meditation Bill Anderton

Meditation covers the origins, theory and benefits of meditation.
It includes over 30 meditations and provides all the advice you
need to mediate successfully.

Crystal Wisdom Andy Baggott and Sally Morningstar

Crystal Wisdom is a fascinating guide to the healing power of
crystals. It details the history and most popular modern uses of
crystals and vibrational healing. It also covers colour, sound and
chakra healing, and gem, crystal and flower essences.

Celtic Wisdom Andy Baggott

Celtic Wisdom is a dynamic introduction to this popular subject.
The author covers Celtic spirituality, the wisdom of trees,
animals and stones, ritual and ceremony and much more.

Feng Shui Jon Sandifer

Feng Shui introduces the origins, theory and practice of the
Chinese art of perfect placement, or geomancy. It provides
easy-to-follow techniques to help you carry out your own
readings and create an auspicious living space.

The Essential Nostradamus Peter Lemesurier

The Essential Nostradamus charts the life of this extraordinary
man, and includes newly discovered facts about his life and
work. Peter Lemesurier unravels his prophecies for the coming
decades.

New titles

Psychic Awareness   Cassandra Eason

Psychic Awareness is a fascinating guide to using the power of your mind to enhance your life. Simple exercises will develop your abilities in clairvoyance, telepathy, detecting ghosts, dowsing and communicating with a spirit guide.

Reiki   Penelope Quest

Reiki explains the background to this healing art and how it can improve your physical health and encourage personal and spiritual awareness and growth. Discover how simple Reiki is to use, whether for self-healing or treating other people.

Kabbalah   Paul Roland

Kabbalah is an accessible guide to the origins, principles and beliefs of this mystical tradition. It includes original meditations and visualisations to help you gain higher awareness and understanding.

Colour Healing   Pauline Wills

Colour Healing explains the vital role colour plays in your physical, emotional and spiritual well-being and how it is used in healing. Meditations and practical exercises will help you to discover the vibrational energies of all the colours of the rainbow.

Tibetan Buddhism   Stephen Hodge

Tibetan Buddhism explains the basic teachings and central concepts of Tibetan Buddhism. There is also guidance on basic meditation, the nature of offerings and worship, and the requirements for embarking on Tantric practice.

Maya Prophecy   Dr Ronald Bonewitz

Maya Prophecy is an intriguing introducting to the prophetic warnings for the future from one of the greatest early civilisations. It explores how Maya religion, mathematics and the Maya calendar provide support for the veracity of the prophecy, and how you should prepare for what lies ahead.